CW00498330

Dictionary
for the Idle

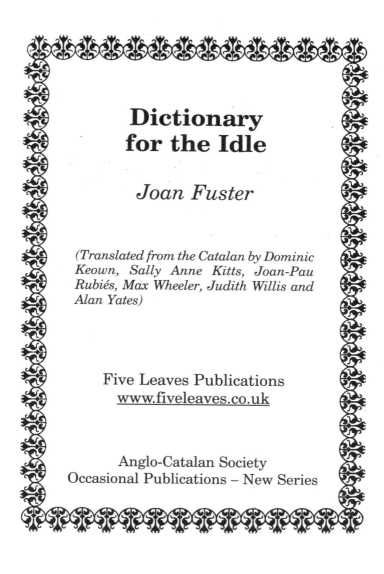

Dictionary
for the Idle

Joan Fuster

*(Translated from the Catalan by Dominic
Keown, Sally Anne Kitts, Joan-Pau
Rubiés, Max Wheeler, Judith Willis and
Alan Yates)*

Five Leaves Publications
www.fiveleaves.co.uk

Anglo-Catalan Society
Occasional Publications – New Series

Dictionary for the Idle

This edition published in 2006
by Five Leaves Publications,
PO Box 8786, Nottingham NG1 9AW
info@fiveleaves.co.uk, www.fiveleaves.co.uk

in association with
the Anglo-Catalan Society

We would like to thank the Institut Ramon Llull,
Generalitat de Catalunya, the Càtedra Joan Fuster,
University of Valencia, Grup 62, and the heirs of Joan
Fuster for their support of this project.

©The Estate of Joan Fuster

Translation
©Dominic Keown, Sally Anne Kitts, John-Pau Rubiés,
Max Wheeler, Judith Willis and Alan Yates

Introduction ©Dominic Keown

ISBN: 1905512066

Five Leaves acknowledges financial support
from Arts Council England

Contents

Introduction

A Question of Format

Perhaps the most surprising feature of this apparently innocuous volume is the title whose banality is both unusual and intriguing. There are few publications which could offer less inducement to be read than a wordbook; and an assumed indolence on the part of the reader hardly implies, in turn, engagement with issues of interest or moment. The explanation for such anomalous self-deprecation is best understood, of course, in the historical context of a repressive dictatorship. An important function of Franco's censorship was to impose a single *national* unity by proscribing all vestiges of language and culture which might challenge Castilian, the officially imposed idiom. In this way, though written in Catalan and thereby illegal, the subservience implicit in the title suggests that this opuscule should be taken as no threat to the cultural hegemony of Spanish or the moral authority of the regime. If anything its presence would merely serve to confirm the status quo — that is, the subsidiary irrelevance of the vernacular — and could thereby be tolerated.

There can be little doubt that Fuster belittled the importance of his work precisely for this reason. After all, as far as the censor was concerned, it would be absurd to imagine that a dictionary for those with nothing better to do could constitute any threat to the rigidly imposed stability of Franco's regime and the enforced pre-eminence of its official language.

There is, however, a much weightier dimension which belies the putative superficiality of this project. Fuster was an inveterate Gallophile and it is not difficult to discern in his dictionary the guiding influence of the Enlightenment and, in particular, the encyclopedic movement. Indeed, the similarity is not only evident in the adoption of the model

1

of a lexicon as a basis for intellectual speculation but the struggle of the *philosophes* against the censorship and obscurantism of an absolute monarchy and regressive church had also much in common with the Catalan resistance to the similarly reactionary mindset of this most fanatically religious of dictatorships.

As such, it is by no means difficult to see Voltaire's acutely incisive *Dictionnaire Philosophique* as the inspiration for the project. Fundamental to the stylistics of the original enterprise is a tension in the discourse whose mixture of ironic flippancy and erudition sought to sharpen the critical instinct in the reader as regards the correct interpretation of the information provided. And Fuster's extraordinary book, devised in a configuration largely unknown in contemporary literatures, exploits the same strange combination of aphoristic frivolity and irony, on the one hand, and serious deliberation on the other. The application of wit and humour to scupper the presumptuous and pious values of the Establishment is a commitment shared by both authors. The devilment implicit in the exercise in the debunking of official values, for example, is evident in the format itself where the 'fortuitous' arrangement of alphabetical order will compromise the sanctity of key elements of the social fabric. In this way, a concept of the magnitude of majesty may be deflated through the locating of its meagre definition next to a comparatively voluminous explication of, say, mayonnaise!

As such, the hybridity of the dictionary encourages the reader to separate the intellectual wheat from the chaff as the genial satirist's intent resounds throughout as evident in his favoured device: "Les livres les plus utiles sont ceux dont les lecteurs font eux-memes la moitié".[1]

The tension between seriousness of purpose and superfluous flourish involves a flexibility of thought shared by author and reader which will act in itself as a counter to the blind acceptance of the pedestrian dogmatism imposed by the regime. As a consequence, the capacity to read between the lines becomes essential for the correct assimilation of the enterprise, as is made apparent from the very start with tongue very much in cheek.

> From the very first line I want to disabuse you, the reader, as to the scope of the title of the book you have in your hands. It was not my intention — need I explain? — to compile a dictionary. As on other occasions, I am merely gathering in one volume an incoherent series of writings, diverse in theme and unequal in length, which may be categorized within the modest yet elastic genre of the essay.

Despite the author's protestations to the contrary, the transparent flippancy of much of the discourse belies a critical intent to which the reader must become attuned. These are no "diverse" and "incoherent" jottings but a carefully disguised ideological attack on the closed and repressive mindset of Francoism. Indeed, the terseness of the sophistication becomes evident in one of the central narrative strategies. To avoid the undesired involvement of the censor, the locus of the meditation is necessarily fixed somewhere removed in the fields of history, literature, science or international current affairs. However, it is the reader's responsibility to recognise how the thrust of the argument returns inevitably to the despicable system controlling Spain. Paradoxically, then — and despite the implication of the title — we cannot allow ourselves to be idle for a second as the work becomes exemplary of "*faire penser*", the *philosophes* ultimate aim of stimulating reflection as a first step to resistance.[2]

*Those who can make you believe absurdities can
make you commit atrocities*

Voltaire

In a manner entirely similar to Nazi Germany and Fascist
Italy, the Franco regime was predicated on a series of par-
tial and tendentious interpretations of history which,
together with a discreditable recourse to myths, lent spurious justification to its execrable designs. Though less
inimical than the new Roman Empire of the Fascists or
the Aryan supremacy of the Nazis, there was no shortage
of the same messianistic purpose in Spanish *Caudillismo*.
In familiar autocratic fashion, the divinely inspired nature
of the *Generalísimo*'s crusade against democracy was pro-
claimed far and wide from every official quarter but may
be illustrated pertinently by the legends on the coinage
which rejoiced in the anointed victor of the Civil War,
"*Francisco Franco, Caudillo de España por la gracia de
Dios*" (Francisco Franco, *Caudillo* of Spain by the Grace of
God).

As was the case with Italy and Germany, the no less
despicable imperialist spirit was also pervasive and evident in the device on the flip side whence from the fascis-
tic war cry resounded with equal numismatic pretension,
"*España, Una, Grande y Libre*" (Spain, One, Great and
Free). Needless to say, the "greatness" and "freedom" perceived in an economic backwater whose chaotic loss of
empire and disastrous policy of autarky was rivalled only
by its total disrespect for human rights and rule of justice
merely serves to underline the maniacal irrelevance typical of the abomination of Francoism. Equally spurious, of
course, was the obsessive view of an irrefutable *national*
unity which allegedly conjoined a geographical area which
boasts one of the richest ethno-linguistic mosaics in
Europe, each element imbued with a consciousness of historical difference and the legitimacy of their claim for
autonomy.

4

As such, if prevented by censorship from directly criticising the specious partiality of such fatuous speculation Fuster could at least ridicule by analogy the mindset which would promote and accept such spurious argument. And it is precisely the imposition and acceptance of the official version, metanarrative or explanation — in generic terms initially yet with clear relation to the specifics of Spain — which the essayist subverts with such poignant humour. Indeed, his first definition will establish a trajectory which will be continued throughout the work: that is to say, an insistent exposing of the use of myth in the fabrication of ideological purpose.

Fuster begins his analysis — in the Catalan edition — with a meditation on one of the central and most unquestioned values of our society: we refer, of course, to the concept or construct of love. As we all know so well, this topic is inescapable in the modern western world and we are incessantly bombarded with examples of its pervasive influence throughout the media: from Hollywood to the Gospels, the Hit Parade and glossy magazines, art and literature. However, with systematic reference to La Rochefoucauld and Engels, Fuster evolves a convincing theorem which indicates that this emotive passion might not necessarily be an intrinsic force, as we are led to believe, but is better understood simply as a "twelfth-century invention."

According to Fuster's scrutiny, after its construction and promotion by the troubadors, love's dynamic charge spread so pervasively through Europe — mainly through the power of the written word — that it came to condition completely the sensitivity of the West. So much so that its fundamental social relevance is rarely even questioned — as may be exemplified by our bland compliance with the Beatles' exhortation that "love is all we need." Accordingly, Fuster's sceptical conclusion, refreshingly ironic in its non-conformism, offers the conviction that in the course of the last millennium European man and woman

5

have been "making love, falling in love, in accordance with the dictates of poets; without realising it, naturally, and without even having read them."

Right from the first, then, the subtext of this extraordinary dictionary becomes patent. In the face of the brainwashing exercised by those irrefutable pillars of western society — with all the interpellative force of the Ideological State Apparatuses identified so lucidly by the post-Marxist philosopher Louis Althusser — it is essential for the individual to remain constantly vigilant with a well-honed critical faculty in order to discern correctly the tendentious intent.[3] Or, as Montserrat Lunati puts it elegantly in her study of Quim Monzó's critical instinct — which might be equally well applied to Fuster — the author should "first and foremost revise those concepts considered untouchable by a culture which accepts as universal and natural criteria which are not this at all since they have been socially constructed."[4] This is all the more relevant in Spain, of course, where Franco's hegemonic message was propagated and imposed with such cynical repression.

The full relevance of the deliberation, however, may be more readily perceived in the second definition. "Fate" which offers speculation in the more closely-related area of historiography. In a gloss on another of one of Voltaire's familiar anecdotes Fuster exposes in customary malicious manner — and with a *reductio ad absurdum* worthy of the master — the illegitimacy of the adducement of myths for historical interpretation. The example selected refers to Cleopatra's nose which, according to the legend about to be discredited, was the motive behind many a battle between lusty Roman generals of the classical era.

Despite the distance of its reference, the pertinence of this speculation to Franco's Spain and beyond is readily apparent. Not only does the dictator fit the bill of a Latin martial ruler — a *Generalísimo*, no less — but his directorate in turn based its justification on the myth of the crusade for the salvation of a fatherland whose messianic mission would sanction the abomination of *Caudillismo*. Needless to say, the pertinence of such diversionary fabrication sounds more than a little familiar in the world of today when other such Cleopatra's noses like the imaginary Weapons of Mass Destruction disguise the interest of petro-dollars; and engagements which are termed Operation Infinite Justice disclose a self-righteousness of purpose which, as with the Egyptian queen's proboscis, conveniently ignores much of the actual historical detail of the origins of the belligerence.

The Methodology of Reason

Throughout the work, the style of the deliberation becomes entirely organic with respect to the communication of authorial purpose as Fuster's elaborative discourse is exemplary in its scientific basis. As Shakespeare would have it we are repeatedly impressed by a "dependence of thing upon thing" in the reasoned adducement of data and its subsequent analysis, a phenomenon which, in itself, embodies the antithesis of the spurious fabrication so typical of the regime. The apparently fatuous selection of the topic of a chair as object for consideration provides a pertinent example. With a detailed historical study of this most mundane of elements the author is able to relate its comparative discomfort value to a corresponding world view which, through a desire for conservation of the regressive status quo in religious and social terms, had a vested interest in keeping humanity deprived of rest and relaxation in this divinely ordained vale of tears.

Evidently there is much humour in such a process which, through the observation and study of the most insignificant of objects, can elicit conclusions of such magnitude. Intellectual curiosity is, however, part and parcel of the investigative instinct and, taking nothing for granted, will rather seek a satisfactory explanation for phenomena: an example of the critical faculty Fuster was so keen to establish and exercise in the face of blind acceptance required by the regime. The preference for aphorisms also ties in nicely with such speculation. In the face of the totalising monolith of Francoist metanarrative the punning and paradoxical enigma of these pithy reflections offers a subversively humorous counterpoint to the seriousness and ruthless simplicity of the official pronouncements.[5]

More weighty in tone — though again hauntingly familiar despite the distance of its reference — is the meditation on justice. With reference to the premature release of two war criminals in France, the author questions accordingly the legitimacy of the continued imprisonment of other offenders whose misdemeanours were paltry in comparison. Despite its chronological precision — the date is specified as the second fortnight of January, 1963 — the speculation has a peculiar relevance if we recall not only the case of General Pinochet and his evasion from trial for torture and assassination but also the release of perpetrators of similar desperate acts in accordance with the peace process in the north of Ireland.

After a long and informed exposition Fuster concludes by isolating the qualitatively different nature of both types of crime. The transgression committed by the German soldiers occurred during the extraordinary circumstance of war. As such, in a normal world it would be highly unlikely for them to offend and now, in peace time, any such relapse would also be improbable. For this reason they may be granted clemency ahead of the petty offender for whom crime tends to be habitual and thus constitutes a constant threat to society and its authority. Though the author considers the net result scandalous his line of argument remains convincing.

Once the insistence on the date is taken into account, however, the whole affair adopts a more positive hue and its specific relevance to Spain becomes more apparent. At this time, when the powers that be were preparing the festivities to commemorate a quarter of a century of Francoist peace (read victory and oppression) Fuster clearly had in mind the wider political dimension of the civic response in the post-dictatorship. In this respect, the drift of his speculation clearly recognises the restoration of social cohesion as essential for the consolidation of the future democracy. Therefore, despite the justness of an enterprise which would bring torturers and murderers to task, the essayist is keen to avoid the danger of retrospective retribution which would merely continue the circle of recrimination and perpetuate the abject social polarisation so typical of the regime. In this way — and despite the sacrifice involved — the prospect of communal division counselled tolerance and clemency as the greater good. The nature of the deliberation is quite remarkable as, more than a decade before Franco's death and with characteristic perception and clarity of purpose, Fuster was among the first to advocate the policy of consensus and inclusion which was to characterise the politics of the Left during the successful Transition to democracy.

The Role of the Individual

There is, nonetheless, a hauntingly emotive dimension to this dictionary which acts as an evocative counterpoint to the academic cerebrality and irony of much of the deliberation. In many ways, as an individual, Fuster was a geoliterary exile in terms of language and experience. Though remaining in his own environment he was an isolated figure unable to write directly in his language and obliged to locate his deliberation abroad both in terms of physicality and abstraction. Unusually, however, the exteriority of the reference leads to the impression, not of divergence, but rather of the identity of the experience at home and abroad. As has been repeatedly seen, in many ways over there becomes over here and is thus reminiscent of the debate on the topic of the self-in-other and other-in-self so emotively posited by the speculation on *Heimat* by writers such as Freud and Kristeva. In this respect the sense of exile and the individual which pervades the work also offers a evocative personal response to the deliberation on matters of a more institutional character.

There is, for example, a poignantly vulnerable sense of exclusion, difference or not being understood which might be exemplified by the definition of Interest. Here the author is wounded by a companion's incredulity at his fascination with ancient tomes, a sentiment which is conveyed in the astonished phrasing of the interrogative "Are you *really* interested in that?" Similarly, in *Flâner*, the mood becomes more emotively lyrical with the arrival of a friend, an "eloquent and cultured shop-keeper", of the most normal appearance imaginable.

Beneath this petty bourgeois exterior, however, lurks the most unconventional clandestine spirit which, as the tradesman recalls his years spent in Paris, reflects with accumulated nostalgia upon a previous existence as a Baudelairian *flâneur*. At this emotional juncture the author and his habitual cerebral sharpness dissipate as his companion — with his aspirations for personal fulfilment now imprisoned in the guise of a tradesman — celebrates nostalgically the French metropolis with its marginalised artists, *ateliers*, absinthe drinkers and *flâneurs*. Not only does this intensely personal reminiscence offer wistful resistance to the homogenising pressure typical of the regime, it is also recalls of much Satrean deliberation on the ontology of existence in the capitalist system. Time and again the philosopher illustrates, with reference to cocktail waiters, grocers and other similarly banal walks of life, the sense of human banishment implicit in a configuration which, refusing any fulfilment on a personal level, imposes a career on an individual as a means of social identification and incarceration.[6]

In this way, despite its innocuous appearance, Fuster's dictionary constitutes a major work of resistance. On every level the primacy of the individual or the actuality of ordinary people is privileged over the anonymity of power.

Indeed, the conclusion to the definition of fate gives an understated indication of the vexation experienced by common folk who would prefer to remain aloof from the invented metanarrative of the infinitely just cause and unified, triumphant nation to be allowed instead to dedicate themselves to the simpler and more meaningful project of getting on with their everyday lives.

> If tomorrow technocrats are to be in charge, as the sociologists predict, and if their power is also to be final and all-ensuing, Cleopatra's-nose-syndrome will continue to be a threat to the sweet, colourless and resigned mass of subjects whose only aspiration is to live this life in peace and in God's grace.

And whether the pressure to conform comes in the form of the repression of an autocratic regime, an alienating system or an extrinsic institution which is embraced as proper due to the incessant effect of interpellation, the belligerence of the intellectual will make itself apparent in a struggle to prioritise simply the authenticity and individuality of experience over the impulse to homogenise. The point may be illustrated finally by one of the many aphorisms so dear to the author's heart precisely because of their specific, immediate and anecdotal reference in the face of the generic anonymity of the externally imposed directive: "In Madrid newspaper editors write and play politics talking about We, the Spaniards...' In Sueca, people work and harvest rice."[7]

Dominic Keown
November 2005

---

[1] Voltaire, *Dictionnaire Philosophique* (Garnier Flamarion: Paris, 1964) p. 24.

[2] The liberating potential enjoyed by the reader as imagined by Voltaire in his foreword "ce livre n'exige pas une lecture suivie;

mais a quelque endroit qu'on l'ouvre on trouve de quoi réfléchir" finds clear resonance in Fuster's speculation. *Dictionnaire Philosophique* p. 24.

[3] The key piece of work in this respect is, "Ideology and Ideological State Apparatuses" in *Lenin and Other Philosophical Essays* (London: NLB, 1971), pp. 121-73.

[4] Montserrat Lunati, "Quim Monzó i el cànon occidental", *Journal of Catalan Studies*, 1999 (http://www.uoc.es/jocs/2/articles/index.html).

[5] For a more detailed illustration of the subversive effect of humour in the face of the seriousness of the official message see Bakhtin's seminal study, *Rabelais and his World* (Bloomington: Indiana University Press, 1984).

[6] The relevant speculation can be found in Jean Paul Sartre, *Being and Nothingness: An Essay on Phenomenological Ontology* (London: Methuen, 1957).

[7] The episode, no doubt, explains Fuster's decision to entitle his *opus magnum* on the history of his people as *Nosaltres, els valencians* (We, the Valencians) thus challenging the centralist indoctrination effected by the victors of the Civil War in Spain.

Foreword

From the very first line I want to disabuse you, the reader,
as to the scope of the title of the book you have in your
hands. It was not my intention — need I explain? — to
compile a dictionary. As on other occasions, I am merely
gathering in one volume an incoherent series of writings,
diverse in theme and unequal in length, which may be categorised within the modest yet elastic genre of the essay.
In *Figures de Temps*/Figures of Time, (Barcelona, 1957),
and *Indagacions Possibles*/Possible Inquiries (Mallorca,
1958), I cobbled together a little collection of aphoristic
left-overs, in small sections which were relatively or
remotely united in their content. In this case, neither of
these procedures was open to me. The texts grouped in
this volume date from many scattered periods and only
with some violence could they tolerate classification on the
grounds of subject matter. It is for this reason, therefore,
and with the aim of keeping at least the appearance of reg-
ularity, I opted for a third, more comfortable solution: to
title each entry with a key word and then arrange them all
in alphabetical order. This trick is not, of course, new in
any way; but rather boasts of some illustrious precedents.
So much the better. In any case, to vary slightly the nature
of the dictionary, and in order to reduce any supposed
ambitious resonance, I rounded off the name with an
ironic indication of those for whom it is intended: the idle.
The reader should not take this too badly for when all is
said and done it isn't really a lie since when are we going
to read, if not in a moment of idleness? What is more,
although professional writers may affirm that the aspirations of literature are lofty and transcendental, there is no
doubt it has another more vulgar and immediate aim: to
fill the idle moments of hypothetical readers. At least, the
type of literature I cultivate — subordinate, marginal,
homespun literature — cannot embrace aspirations of any

great haughtiness. What I include here are essays: nothing much, really. If, from time to time, they acquire an inflated, dogmatic aspect, it is not intentional: in fact they deal with everyday problems, my own at least, which are precisely those topics that would crop up in a friendly chat between the reader and myself should we ever meet face to face. I hope something or other will be of interest. I myself will be happy if I don't spoil your moment of leisure, or bother you in any significant way.

Joan Fuster
Sueca,
April 3, 1963

ACCOMPLICE
An accomplice is anyone who helps you to be as you are.

AVARICE
I suspect that there must have been a change in the quality of the psychological condition of avarice. I can't speak from my own experience since, not being what you might call prodigal, I've never considered myself to be over-dominated by an urge to covet material goods. However, I think the point I make can be deduced from a number of obvious observations. This curious, deadly sin called avarice is, if I am not mistaken, something more than a mere exacerbation of a possessive instinct. Technically, perhaps that's all it is: an inordinate appetite (*inordinate*, as a moralist would term it) for riches. In spite of this, in practice, we only really label as avaricious those people who combine a more or less active propensity to acquire with a voluptuous view of economic wealth. Let me express myself better. I think that execrable gold fever in itself is not enough to determine the presence of avarice: the chrematistically famished individual must also necessarily have the sensitivity of a *gourmand*.

There are many, many people who strive to augment their fortune to extremes of stupendous aberration yet we would never dare accuse them of avarice. The fixation with acquiring wealth is perfectly compatible with an almost bromidic indifference for the material value of money. In general, the rich man views his wealth in terms of the social power it confers on him; systematic saving, even meanness, can and very often does obey a simple sense of cautiousness. Certain types of capitalist enterprises, in the

15

areas of industry and finance, are mere professional expansion which grow with the impulse of inertia in the mechanisms of the system and in which profit is nothing more than a routine consequence. The passion for land acquisition, so characteristic of the agrarian world, also supposes some element of voluptuousness, but one projected onto things, that is, onto the soil, and not onto money itself. It is money that polarises a type of sensual frenzy.

The amount doesn't really matter. On occasions avarice springs from quantities which are ridiculously meagre. But insignificant or large, these sums will never escape the miser's grasp: he is a retainer. His reluctance to part with money does not derive so much from a fear of dissipation or superfluous expense as from an anxiety to keep hold of his cash to enjoy it in his own way; and for this reason, it has to be cash. Ultimately, it has everything to do with making a fetish out of currency. I have no idea what historians will make of this but I imagine that avarice did not appear as a form of human conduct until society instituted in its economic life an autonomous medium to facilitate the exchange of goods, to wit, currency. Before this moment, in a context of primary economics of direct exchange the miser would appear to be unimaginable.

We could not even conceive of him in the early stages of subsequent development when, for example, man uses man, in the figure of the slave, as a primitive material of currency. It is cash, nothing more nothing less; real money, made of metal and as such a precious substance, which is the prime mover of this vice. For the miser, money is not a means of acquisition or dominance, or a neutral sign of economic worth, but the absolute reality of this value. Doubtlessly he is partly right, since gold and silver have for centuries actually had an immanent value — the maximum immanent value in the field of economic relations. It is precisely this: gold and silver — gold and silver, in cash — that the miser longs to have. In cash, since for him this provides metal's supreme guarantees.

The popular image of the miser — that fabricated by folklore and the stage — usually includes two qualities incidental to the one described above: stinginess and usury. On the one hand, he is reticent in the face of any possible expenditure; on the other, he makes loans on ignominious terms. Both traits tend to highlight in the figure of the miser certain facets primordially susceptible to exploitation in a satiric or dramatic attack. "One day the barber cut his fingernails; so he picked up all the clippings and took them away", says a character in Plautus's *Aulularia* with reference to Euclio the Miser. Molière's Harpagon, a direct descendant of Euclio, besides being as mean as his predecessor, lends money at 28 per cent and with certain ridiculously opprobrious, supernumerary conditions.

Plautus and Molière wrote comedies, that is, caricatures. Be that as it may, their depictions of the miser are not wholly inexact. However, to a greater extent than usury or stinginess, the pathetic fervour with which the miser treats his money must be considered a more accurate symptom of avarice. This is the distinctive quality of the figure. In traditional verses, children's stories, comic strips, the model is repeated assiduously. We see the ambitious old man, excited, smiling with a glint of madness in his eyes, in the darkest corner of the house, counting and recounting his treasure. He touches his coins, dotes on and caresses them with a fixed, insatiable avidity which can only be described as lascivious. It forms a strange spectacle, of course, and just because it is so strange, perhaps too strange, we feel inclined to label it inaccurate. Nonetheless, we are required to accept it as not merely a possibility but, in fact, quite logical.

If the miser doesn't need to spend his money, what can he be expected to do with it? Gaze upon it, touch it with that morose delectation that is censured by these more severe. Gaze on it and touch it, to feel that it is his in a type of libidinous and effusive manner. You know what Monsieur Grandet used to do at the end of his life:

17

Eugénie piled up his louis on the table and the old gent spent hour upon hour with his eyes fixed on the coins like little children who, when they see for the first time, gaze stupidly at the same object. Grandet, like a small child, smiled in a distressing type of way. "It's all come back to me!", he often exclaimed, as if it were some kind of consummate bliss.

This consummate bliss was the avarice of the cobbler of Saumur, not his meanness in underfeeding the family or his tricks designed to increase the extent of his patrimony. Balzac sensed it. That sick old person who, with gaze ecstatic is bedazzled by the presence of shining *louis*, is your miser *par excellence*. I find it most significant that Grandet is the last *real* miser produced by modern literature. Grandet lived in an age — the first third of the nineteenth century — when it was not difficult to be a miser. His fortune was made up basically of tenancies, mortgages, business, paper money. Naturally, cash — the noble metal — remained, still, unquestionably supreme. But capitalism was progressing and the network of financial dealing was becoming more complex. Grandet could see his millions growing but these millions were not being translated into coins of gold.

Throughout the novel, Balzac is keen to point out the preoccupation which has his character continuously on edge: a yearning to possess gold coins. Gold is the obsession which overwhelms him, makes him lose control, and gives him his only delight. Each New Year's Eve, his daughter Eugénie had to show her parents the money which Grandet had given her for one reason or another and which she had to hold on to religiously. The family exhibition of the girl's gold coins, attractive and specially selected, was the main feast for the miser. That was still the case in Grandet's time; it would not be so as the century progressed. A Grandet a hundred years later — on the eve of the Great War — would have to content himself with less tempting fare: bank notes. Gold — normal gold currency — tended to disappear into thin air. And after that silver, which would lose its charms but not because it was second best.

We are now at the point where we must ask ourselves whether or not avarice might simultaneously have undergone some change in its psychological structure. Will it continue to have the same quality if gold and silver are replaced by paper. When those in control of public finance, through intrinsic demands on the system, withdraw currency based on precious metals and circulate in their stead documents of strict promissory value, what possibility of sensual joy is there left for the miser? It must be agreed that a huge pile of notes must also delight, but between the old, glistening *louis* and modern printed paper there is bound to be a decisive difference to the eyes and fingers of the niggard.

Covetousness, his own covetousness, is frustrated in its most delicate aspect. Bank notes are also cash — the miser never questions that. It is merely that it is cash deprived of material consistency: incapable of being physically possessed, just like love letters in place of the tangible presence of the lover. Obviously, we can still picture the old man — we always see the miser as old, as the *topos* decrees — with chiselled features and gleaming eyes, fingering and thumbing a wad of notes, satisfied by their touch and sound. We can picture him but with difficulty. Those rich with paper money and contemporary with banks tend to use current accounts. The great coveters of today don't even have the opportunity of flicking their fingers through the notes except for quantities relevant to domestic consumption. Cheques, shares, numbers written on the subtlest of documents, is what richness means for them. The wealth of the rich man today comes to him via symbolic references. Names and signatures, and nothing more. Could he still be a miser in these conditions? I doubt it.

In any case, if the answer is yes, we would be forced to conclude that avarice today has become, if you'll forgive the expression, algebraic. The pleasure — for pleasure is what it's all about — derived from the possession of money will no longer be a sensual pleasure, as in the days when gold was currency. It will be a restrictively intellectual pleasure. Will it still be worthwhile calling it avarice? Dear me! What a problem!

BEAUTY

I don't think that the ancient and respectable philosopher was right when he said there is nothing so pleasant as the contemplation of beauty without concupiscence. That is the idea of an old or impotent man — old, impotent and happy to be so. For if, when we look upon an adorable body we do not feel the concupiscence which makes us desire it, will we not rather feel anger at not feeling it, or envy of those who feel it? I've still not reached the age when I might be condemned by nature to such a fearful lack of appetite. However, should I reach it one day I would consider myself most unfortunate. Concupiscence — though moralists may say what they like — is life.

C

CHAIR

Verification is easy enough: all you need to do is thumb through a history — illustrated, of course — of furniture. This could be ratified, immediately, by a visit to any museum of figurative painting or the lesser arts where, both in image or in reality, testimonies of the forms of seating used by our forebears are preserved. Nowadays, in many houses of these latitudes, perhaps even in the majority, we will still find many significant models of chairs. The conclusion will already have been drawn by the reader. Western man, so rich and inventive in certain things — mythology, metaphysics, literature, art, war, oppression, and so forth — has shown throughout the centuries a singular lack of imagination for all that refers to his most immediate form of comfort.

It is not merely a question of chairs but the case of chairs is an especially visible indication. It seems, in fact, as though our people have always sat on artefacts whose primary characteristic has been their inhospitable form. It is almost as if for century after century no one has noticed that, in general, the act of sitting responds to a need to rest and that this relief depends on the position of the body. With backs which are more or less perpendicular, flat bottoms and inconceivable dimensions, chairs — and the seats which have succeeded them with each generation of our society — seem to have been built without that elementary requirement being taken into account. Sitting down in a gothic chair must have been torment, or something akin to it. Sitting in a Victorian chair did not indicate, when all is said and done, too energetic a form of progress.

Obviously, progress had actually been made in the form

of improvements. We might be led to believe, however, that these improvements were not the fruit of a rational, methodical solution to the problems encountered. The inclination of the torso of the sitter, the greater or lesser freedom of the legs, the adequate bending of the knees, all are contributing factors to the muscular relaxation which is sought when sitting in a chair. As the evolution of furniture unwinds throughout history, we can see that slowly but surely there was a growing awareness about the optimum facilities for the desired repose being achieved in the best possible way. A slight difference of inches in the height of the legs or in the angle of the back can determine a chair's real quality, or lack of it. However, I reiterate that all that up to recently has been achieved in this respect has not been the result of any rigorous calculation, or, if you will, scientific approach. Rather it seems that the advantages arrived, not unlike decanting, from the passing and unconscious empiricism of the user. They may, however, have come not from the users as much as from exceptional and sporadic flights of the imagination introduced into their route by carpenters and workers with mahogany. Subsequently citizens with economic power, magnates of some opulence, well-off corporations, for example, decided to improve their furniture in proportion to their wealth; this was done, however, without any regard for comfort but for decoration, which is not the same thing. Their concern was with decoration, or the sumptuousness of the material. Palace chairs were made of the most noble wood, of subtle dimensions and sumptuous coverings but, despite everything, they were no more comfortable than chairs in the poorest of houses. It was, I repeat, like this for centuries.

Fortunately, the panorama is changing today. The homes of our well-off friends and furniture in shop windows offer us examples of some really admirable seating. Not just impressive or expensive, but comfortable. With such domestic instruments within our reach, family life will gain in stability. There will be less conjugal dissent and neighbours can drop affectionately by without running the risk of passing the time of day in rigid, demoralising positions. This is real progress as chairs are now made by specialists who know their stuff. But if we stop for a moment to analyse the structure and secret of these beneficent modern chairs, we will be amazed to find out that, in essence, it's like the question of the earth being round and not flat: how come no one thought of it sooner? The question seems slightly ingenuous, but it's not. Undoubtedly, in the confection of furniture nowadays we use products and machinery that only the latest technology could provide. Nonetheless, that is not the decisive factor. The trick behind the perfect chair or seat does not depend on its natural ingredients but on its design. It's a question of invention; and it is curious that man has taken so long to make up his mind to apply himself to these articles of everyday use.

I have already hinted that the chair has not been the only thing to suffer from such considerable retardation. There are important items, of marvellous utility, whose appearance remained reserved for the fullness of the twentieth century. It was only the late maturing of science and a final development of industrialisation which made them possible. To illustrate this in a discreetly grotesque fashion television, jets, radar, iron lungs, etc., were inventions which were not accessible to man of the Middle Ages or Renaissance. I am of the opinion, however, that no great scientific budget would be required to design a comfortable chair and that any old artisan had the skill to produce it. I do not wish to exaggerate and I don't claim that any carpenter of yore could have fashioned chairs like some we see today with their high-wire designs and unimaginable supports. I am merely trying to point out that carpenters of old were equipped enough to try something similar, at least in their willingness to afford the maximum relaxation and most felicitous comfort for their customers; but this willingness was never given a chance, perhaps, because of the lack of demand on the part of the customer for real comfort. This lack of interest may surprise us. We are accustomed to pampering our bodies as much as we possibly can. However, this affection for one's own body is, in effect, a relatively new attitude within our civilisation. Traditionally, virtue was taken to be uncomfortable: austerity, abstinence and mortification. Man's life on this earth was considered an act of sacrifice. Now everyone thinks differently. It's because of this, I'm sure, that we now have comfortable chairs at our disposal — as well as other things.

CHARACTEROLOGY
At determined moments in our life we all begin to look something like a gargoyle.

CHARLATAN
Homme libre, toujours tu chériras la mer! The line — by Baudelaire — is a pretty one: it could almost be by Victor Hugo! All the same... I believe it probable that no Mediterranean man would be sincere if he connected the idea of freedom with the idea of the sea. Perhaps, in part, because the people from this area regard the sea — the adventurous and tempting sea — with a certain distrust. But also, without doubt, because our model of freedom is very particular. For us, in fact, freedom is inseparable from the land — facing the sea — where we have our roots. What is more, it is inseparable from the village square in which we live. I say the square: it could be the agora, the forum, if you prefer certain decorative allusions. Mediterranean society, right up until the present time, has organised itself into cities: we have yet to attain nationhood — I formulate it, like everything, *cum grano salis*. In a city, the collective heart is the square. The widespread and united family of the Mediterranean is nothing more than that, a collection of squares, agoras or forums, open to the proximity of the sea. I believe it unnecessary to transcribe here

the list of place names to justify this, which in any case is clearly predictable. What about freedom, then? Freedom, in the square, in the agora, in the forum, is simply the freedom to converse. When Mediterranean people talk of freedom, they mean nothing more than this. Mediterranean people carry a political chatter box inside them. It is a silenced political chatterbox. Enthusiasts when it comes to gossip, practitioners of the vice of idle chatter, we admire those who excel at it. For that reason the Mediterranean is, essentially, a fertile quarry of tribunes: plebeian tribunes in some cases, or tyrannical tribunes in others. But always tribunes: orators, gossips, charlatans. From Demosthenes or Cicero to Blasco Ibáñez or Mussolini, any silver tongue steals our heart. More than doctrine or intention, we admire loquaciousness. However limited our eloquence, we will always try to make speeches. We enjoy making them as much as listening to them. A foreigner may remind us that perhaps in no other part of the civilised world have there been so many tyrants, throughout history, as there have here. The foreigner would be right. The despot is such a beloved character to us that he almost belongs, so to speak, to folklore. But the Mediterranean dictator cannot escape from the fatality of his native soil: he is just one more gossip, one more charlatan. The transcripts of the speeches of local dictators, from Classical Greece onwards, form a highly notable part of the literary anthologies of the natural or rhetorical languages of the Mediterranean basin. In other places, authoritarianism relies on other merits: providentialism, dynasty, ferocity, a heroic profile, doctrinaire dogma. Whatever the case, we respond with the typical — and commonplace — perorative faculty. To a large extent, the historical dynamism of our societies centres on the freedom to converse: a freedom which the citizens claim as theirs and a monopoly which the tyrants are quick to keep for themselves. A laconic despot would have very little chance of lasting among us. His natural social force — the popular support which he gains — depends on his facility

26

with words. When a good charlatan is in power, everything runs like clockwork. If his administration is deplorable, if as a ruler he is a calamity, he will be redeemed in proportion to his ability to *speak*. In the meantime, everyone else also *speaks*: the subjects, the citizens, the subjugated. The subjects, the citizens and the subjugated do not aspire to lead: they are content to talk, to converse. Sometimes the tyrant concedes them a tolerant opportunity to unburden themselves in mere verbal opposition. On other occasions, the habitués of the square, of the agora, of the forum come out with witticisms and tales which the despot allows to pass with paternal indulgence. The balance of the opposing eloquence gives paradoxical results. But it all comes to the same thing. Both greater and lesser freedom comes down to the question of speech. And also of authority. To speak — to speak in the square — is our greatest dream. Both as dictators and as subjects, we Mediterraneans want to speak: to converse. So what about the sea? The free man always *chérira* the square, the agora, the forum.

CLOCKS AND WATCHES

I sometimes think that the widespread use of portable watches must have been one of the most profound revolutions in the life of modern humanity. A silent, slow revolution, almost imperceptible in its manifestations, but one with subtly pronounced consequences. The average person's sense of time must have changed markedly when they began to have at their disposal the domestic or personal timepiece. The sundial, the hour-glass, other rudimentary procedures for measuring the passage of time were, it seems, external and rigid modes of checking the hours: they never affected the awareness of temporality felt, more or less instinctively, by the individual. The fact that there was an abundant gnomic literature, morbid and admonitory in its message, particularly designed to decorate sundials, amounts to a paradoxical confirmation of that. The typical inscriptions on old sundials recalled the fugitive nature of time and intimations of death: *Cotidie morior, Dum spectas fugio, Maneo nomini, Each hour inflicts a wound, the last one kills, Latet ultima, Ex his una tibi.* This epigraphic material tended to be decorative and was, in any case, ineffective: elliptical Latinisms or concentrated aphorisms, they were not to be read with too much attention, nor did the place where they were displayed lend itself to enhancing their function as solemn reminders, to the detriment of their exemplariness. Belfry clocks, moreover, were hardly more effective in this sense, perhaps even less so. The chiming of public clocks concealed their placable harshness with liturgical resonances, and they amounted to not much more than automatic signals for parsing the people's regular routines. I suspect that things must have become slightly different with the introduction of the wall clock, and that, gradually, the change must have been accentuated with the spread of the pocket watch and, finally, of the wristwatch. We now have instruments for measuring time that are with us throughout the twenty-four hours of the day. We need them to regulate our most important and our most banal activities. At first sight, they seem to be inoffensive, purely utilitarian, artefacts. But the role they play in our lives is without precedent. They bear no high-sounding, philosophical inscriptions. They do not need to: the effect they have is more sharply penetrating than anything that might formerly have been achieved by the severe mottoes on sundials. Present-day people deal with time as did their predecessors: using it, wasting it, killing it, spending it. The difference is that nowadays we have constantly before us an impassive sphere and those incessant hands which measure it out for us, which count it out for us. Modern philosophers have often insisted on the temporal condition of humanity: they have explained to us in academic terms that we are historical, that we are death-bound, and other such things. The watch-making industry, for its part, has contributed greatly to fostering our conviction of such temporality. Whenever we consult our watches we receive a painful shock. We often do not even realise it: it is just a momentary and unconscious impression, a subliminal flash — as people now put it. But it is there all the same. We check the time to turn up for a meeting, to start a particular job, to catch a train, and really — or simultaneously — the watch just tells us that we are time and that time is running out. In the past people were not subject to this kind of permanent warning. For them, the passage of time took on a less immediate, less specific character: they *felt* it through the cosmic cycles, day and night, the seasons, the rhythm of the harvests and of the animals' breeding. Time, then, was an obscure magma, unfathomable, whose flow was only faintly felt. Now, by contrast, clocks and watches convey time translated into minutes and seconds, into incomprehensibly fleeting fractions. We carry in our hand a severe indicator of the uncertainty of life and of the fatality of death. This is something which has been bound to make us different — slightly different, at least — from our ancestors. That is the revolution of which I spoke at the beginning.

CONVICTION

Every conviction — every serious conviction — will be converted into prejudice by ulterior convictions. Think about it. Each conviction you acquire is a further prejudice you accumulate. You already know what prejudice means: original vice. If you zealously guard your intellectual freedom, if you aspire to preserve the permanent readiness which is its requisite, you should strive to be people of few convictions. The fanatic is an individual who is totally convinced, a person of many convictions. I hardly think that fanaticism is an admirable point of view. Prudence, that cardinal virtue, counsels against such mental and moral exasperations. When all is said and done, you don't need too many convictions to get by in life. Three or four. That's all.

COWARDLINESS

If we have in mind to — and we need to have a mind to — we will always find a reason to excuse the actions of a coward. The reason is simple. Is there anyone among us who has never been afraid? Obviously, fear can be overcome: they say the brave person is merely someone who is afraid but bears it. That may be so. What I do know is there is no humanly possible way to fix a moral limit in this field. Everyone deals with fear in their own way and as God wills them to come to terms with it. Let us not be misled: everyone is a coward in comparison with someone else. You can be as bold as you wish but it will never be impossible that one of your neighbours considers your bravery as inferior to his own and that, as a consequence, considers you a coward. A good rule of thumb, in this as in many other spheres, is this: never criticise or condemn anyone for being what you might be on some occasion. A coward, for example.

CYNICISM

The point is worth reiterating: a good case can be made for cynicism. In essence, that which we call cynicism is nothing more than the antidote for hypocrisy. The diametrical opposite of the cynic is not the virtuous man, or even the puritan: it's the Pharisee.

DEFECT

Defect originally must have meant something akin to deficit and nothing more: some or other type of deficit. The idea of defect is diametrically opposed to the idea of excess: to sin by defect or excess. It is curious, nonetheless, that the majority of excesses usually receive, in everyday language, the label of defects. Deficiency and superabundance are at times — and contradictorily — equivalents. Sins as the saying tells us.

DOING

We are always doing something different from what we were meant to.

DYING

Dying too young is a mistake. Dying too old as well. In general, dying is always a mistake. The trouble is that we could say the same thing about living.

EGOISM
Perhaps inasmuch as we are not egoists we are blessed. And perhaps, as well, inasmuch as we are blessed we are incapable of being egoists.

EPITAPH
For example:

> here lies
> j f
> he died
> as he lived
> unwillingly

ETHICS
When the philosophers and *Aufklärer* of the eighteenth century proposed and preached the idea of progress, they could hardly have imagined to what point posterity, a posterity which had precisely made progress, would mistrust that bounteous optimism which predicted an ever more felicitous and nobler future for humanity. I do not think that the use of the word mistrust is excessive. It is only the reactionary wing of Romanticism and their intellectual heirs that have dared object to or criticise progress in absolutely rigid terms. I do not wish to talk about these but about certain others. It is obvious that the initial euphoria, gratitude and hope projected onto the liberating perspective of progress have waned in enthusiasm and insistence. Progress was not — is not — just a good intention but also a fact and, as it became realised, so one of its most undisputed facets began to arouse suspicions, fear

32

and so on. In practice, progress has come to mean primordially technical progress for everyone: a complicated series of phenomena which has its origins in the theoretical advances of science, has material applications, revolutionises the means of production, extends the possibilities for consumption and the domination of nature. Latterly, this has happened with an intensity and acceleration unprecedented in history. Let us leave to one side for the moment any consideration about social conditioning — an impulse for private gain or collective planning — which set it in motion. The important thing is the magnitude of the process and its repercussions in the whole network of life styles in the modern world. It has in fact achieved a fabulous change in the behaviour and mentality of hundreds of millions of people. The situation created is totally new and this newness both disconcerts and arouses anxieties which end up as distrust: distrust of progress and of technology.

The average person takes no notice of or is insensitive to it. As a rule they accept and use the options offered by applied science — the car and penicillin, television and electric fridge, radar and record player, film and glossy magazines, advances in cybertechnics and synthetic plastics —, everything that's offered, without wondering whether the consequences they bring could be anything more than mere utility. In urban zones of industrial countries, the adaptation of people to the habits imposed by technological expansion has been achieved on a massive scale. The immediate advantages were too readily visible for it to be otherwise; the inflexible force of economics would tolerate no alternative either. It is amidst this docility that cries of alarm are now bring raised. Suspicion and protest, however, are emanating from concrete and unmistakable sectors. They are coming from that field of ideologies usually referred to as humanity — in the form of a case made in favour of humanity. The general and basically explicative thesis says, in a nutshell, progress, or certain deviations in progress, are a threat to the dignity of humanity. Many and varied are the voices that make up

33

this cry of alarm. There is the denouncing of machinery which dehumanises work and implants uniformity and standardisation. There is a cry for individual liberty endangered by those derivatives of progress: the great masses, the drugs of the police and state. There is annoyance bred from the invasion of a contraband culture and the mass media, both exclusively commercial. There is the fear that biological and chemical discoveries — for example, *in vitro* fertilisation or auto-fecundation — might alter the natural structure of human life. There is the tragic experience of the destructive power achieved by the most recent scientific weapons: the nightmare of a nuclear catastrophe is justified and harrowing. The list could go on and on. Literature inspired by this theme is well-known and abundant.

The defenders of humanity in the face of the depravity of technology know, however, not to go too far. Their diatribe against progress comes up against a brick wall of common sense. No ideologue would ever dare condemn technology *en bloc*. They would never do this partly because they are obliged to recognise that, in the last analysis, technology is everything: tying a knot, lighting a fire by rubbing two sticks together, rounding down with a file, just as much as the working of the subtlest electronic brain. Partly also because no one today would have the heart to go without the service of whatever instrument technology places at our disposal: the telephone or linotype, aeroplane or bidet, electric light or lift. Such a radical renunciation would require the heroism of the *Flos Sanctorum* hermits and even the most trenchant detractors, be they bar-room, educated or academic, would never endorse an asceticism which returned them to the Middle Ages or Palaeolithic period. All this would imply stagnation and eventually a return to barbarism. The critics of progress cannot overcome these elementary difficulties and so become tortured, wretched, cautious and fastidious. They will never give a clear no and their reluctance leaves us in a state of complete confusion.

34

However, if their criticism seems hardly solid — even when construed by humanity writers and thinkers who are all well versed in the art of dialogue — the solutions proposed appear no more serious and the criticism remains little more than that: pure criticism, disconsolate in all its impotence. There are only a few well-meaning souls, of a catechistic leaning and secondary intellectual capacity, who have been able to believe in the efficacy of a palliative. They are the supporters of what was once known as moral progress. I say what was once known as since today the label has fallen pitifully into oblivion. I know not if there be still some country priest or provincial journalist who may still be serving it up to his customers. The argument is quite simple. In the face of the acceleration in material progress, a parallel moral progress had to be proposed which acted, if not as a brake at least as a compensatory force. A deep ethical reservoir nullified the real or potential evil of technology. When all is said and done, technology is nothing more than a collection of instruments, a series of means, a group of utensils and, therefore, it is morally neutral. We can make good use of it. It is up to us to make technology work for good or evil, to make it help man improve or deteriorate, stimulate society or corrupt it. At worst, technology can offer execrable temptation, blinding delights, turbulent complications, but we are always able to resist them should we wish. It is through our own will that technology works against us, or casts us into pernicious inebriation. As a consequence, we merely need to hone our moral sense and the threat will be repulsed. Such is the illusion which forms the basis of moral progress.

It seems worthwhile pointing out that the term moral progress sounds like a cliché coined by those progressive souls of the eighteenth century rather than the latter-day sceptics of technology. Until the eighteenth century, no one had ever dared mention progress with reference to morality since the imperative of ethical perfection was considered a static notion. Traditionally, in fact, the ideal

35

of morality was not subject to chance once it had been defined. Within the constancy of a preceptive scheme, concrete and individual realisations acquired a greater or lesser degree of plenitude: there was a mode of conduct defined as perfect — the saint, the wise man, the virtuous man — and one and all were urged to imitate and emulate them. It was not a question of progress, then, but something entirely different. The Enlightenment, on the other hand, began to view the ideal of morality on a dynamic plane. In this age ethics were susceptible to evolution. Indeed, the plurality of ethical codes demonstrated by history, which reveal the customs of different peoples, confirms the possibility of a progression in this field. From the level assumed by philosophers and *Aufklärer* — the level of Reason — earlier moralities seemed like a series of trial runs, frustrated yet still encouraging. From that point onwards, however, when Reason stabilised humanity in its correct position, the road to virtue opened up; its perspectives were inexhaustible. All previous moralities, the norms of stoicism, epicurianism, Buddhism, Christianity, were defective. The morality of Reason was, in essence, definitive: ever predisposed to a further degree of perfection. The ethics of the Enlightenment declared, at least in a latent state, a type of pure simultaneity between progress in its two forms: moral and technological. The preachers of antiprogressive moral progress, however, exclude on principle any rectification of the established ethic and when they speak of moral progress they merely allude to an intensifying of traditional morality. The term progress, in this context, appears as nothing more than a grotesque paradox.

I have insisted on this point of moral progress, though its importance is tenuous and dated, for one simple reason: it takes us to the real heart of the matter. It is not just through chance or rhetoric that those apprehensive of technology have pulled such a strained term of reference for morality from up their sleeve. The morality they postulate has become the first victim of socio-economic upheaval. The eruption of technology, material progress and its consequences have appropriated the ethical system in which people lived the world over and shaken it to the bone. Moreover, irreparably so. Institutions, criteria, taboos, the very concepts of freedom and responsibility, scales of values, the *imago mundi* upon which all this rested, became unsustainable in a society which contradicted or threatened them by the simple fact of its own organisation. We could illustrate this with numerous examples. Let us think, to adduce but one, about the crisis being suffered by the venerable conventions surrounding sex and the family. I will be careful to refrain from contending that today people are more debauched and licentious than at any other time in history. I will not even dare sustain that nowadays the facilities to practice those forms of delight are better than before. That would be merely anecdotal. The changes are more profound and range from birth control to trial marriages, from a weakening in parental authority to the spread of divorce, from the success of psychoanalysis to preoccupation with eugenics, from commercialised corporal exhibitionism in cinema and magazines to the *Kinsey Report*. In the future that progress is preparing for us, neither Don Juan nor Othello will have their place assured: nor Oedipus, nor Madam Bovary, nor Joseph most chaste in the Bible, nor Tristan, nor Juliet, nor the Karamazov troupe. Adultery and jealousy, abusive fatherhood and parricide, incest, continence, courting, tragic passion may still live on, but in a psychological and legal framework very different from those we have known to date. Technology, in creating new conditions of existence, will turn the established moral order on its head.

Surviving humanisms cower before this fact. Their conception of humanity and social bonds is defrauded and belied by the events of every day. The humanists, however, do not discard or rectify their outlook. They still have faith in it. They believe there is a modulus of human dignity, an axiology, a desideratum of intellectual comfort

— their own — that should be preserved, whatever the cost, in the midst of the convulsion of life styles in which we live. They feel that this should be preserved above all else for in it they see the definitive incarnation of an ideal which is also definitive. Perhaps people of all ages have tended to believe that their morality was the best of all possible moralities. We are no exception. Yet, unlike people of earlier ages, we have a more poignant notion of the relativity of our place in time. Historicism has made us fully aware that we are an episode; one more in the long succession of episodes which make up human history. We know that we are relative by comparison with the past and we must accept ourselves as such, with equal reference to the future. The morality which is now in the process of disintegration — the moribund culture in which we live — cannot forget or conceal its mortal condition. Valéry's well known phrase would be apposite here. Nonetheless, we are reluctant, the professional humanists more than anyone, to recognise ourselves as a transitory and perishable civilisation. In other words, while we are witnesses to its death throes we would rather not take notice. Except that progress raises an invincible obstacle, or rather works against us. With progress and morality face to face in such bare-faced altercation, humanisms — that is humanists — do not know what to do. They pretend to ignore that a choice must be made.

There is always someone who wistfully points out that science or technology has gone too far. It's a sterile warning. A science or technology which remained short of its own possibilities would not be, for this reason, a more moral science or technology, but a devalued science or technology. This observation — and I am not the first to make it — is startlingly obvious. Science or technology would not return to the moderating sphere of morality by placing limits on themselves. Nor would they make humanism more secure. What is more, by their very nature science and technology would never resign themselves to self-limitation. They are governed by an intrinsic law which pushes them forever onwards. Each advance in progress — new scientific knowledge or a new technological method — engenders another, and the process appears to have no visible limits. The fantasy of science-fiction writers seems feeble in comparison with calculations worked out seriously in lectures, seminars and laboratories. Verne, Wells and company have had many of their prophecies confirmed although perhaps much more of modern day science fiction, which now strike us as ridiculous, will be an everyday occurrence in the future. In certain works by Jean Rostand we find a great many incredible predictions which the biologist guarantees with all the weight of his authority: procreation of twins at will, ectogenesis, controlled mutations, chemical stimulation of intelligence, artificial parthenogenesis, suspended animation, even the production of a type of superman. Aldous Huxley traced the satiric image of a rigorous, technocratic society in *Brave New World*. According to Rostand, Huxley's tale has now started to become actual reality.

> Is it not a biologised humanity that can count among its own, creatures who have emerged from vitrified semen, in which every day nerve strands of the encephalon are sectioned to modify the psychic personality, wherein hormones are habitually used to produce growth, balance behaviour or sexuality?

What the biologists says here about his science and technology could be said by any other specialist referring to his own. Only the severest cataclysm could ever interrupt this portentous advance. The resulting trauma would take us back to the caves.

Today, science and technology displace or devour anything non-congeneric. Our grandparents'morality will be literally unusable for our grandchildren. We ourselves watch it sinking day by day. A new ethic must apply to a new society: a new culture. The morality of the future will have its roots in those objective pressures created by progress. It cannot be said that contemporary experts in doctrinal matters are hard at work in the task of theorising and defining these tendencies. The disquisitions of today's moralists — the whole gamut of existentialists, for example — seem merely to be the last corruption of a previous morality rather than the starting principle of morality prepared for the imminent brave new world. I make use of the words Huxley chose for the title of his sarcastic work without sharing his pessimism. Huxley is one of these humanists who distrusts progress. Generally speaking, however, we are entitled to higher hopes. The society of the future will not resemble ours too closely: that is not to say that its people will be any less human than their counterparts of ancient societies. Tomorrow, at least, there will be much better opportunities. Science and technology will afford, we are told, a degree of control for the human race never before experienced: control over itself, its species, over things, over the universe. It will be an illustrious opportunity. For our part, it would be niggardly not to believe that we will make good use of it.

FATE

This word, coined by Pascal, struck lucky, and is still used today to underline the intervention of chance in the course of historic events. If Cleopatra's nose had been a little longer or a little shorter, the destiny of the world would have been quite different. As far as it seems, that eminent lady was of shapely dimensions, somewhat scatterbrained and, last but not least, an important queen. Her romantic attachment to various Roman dignitaries must surely have been a bitter pill to swallow for both her contemporaries and her successors alike. A more circumspect or chaste Cleopatra, an uglier Cleopatra, would have played a very different part in the lives of Caesar and Mark Anthony. The politics of Rome — the whole world at that time — would also have been different. Whether Cleopatra's sex-appeal depended on the length of her nose or not is a thing I do not know; it is something, moreover, which is literally negligible. But both popular and educated opinion came to attribute a decisive weight to the flings of the Egyptian queen, as far as the development of certain episodes of Roman imperialism were concerned; and they weren't so very far wrong either. Cleopatra's nasal appendix thus acquired a clearly representative value. For centuries, men of the West would not conceive of the story in any other way. For them, collective life, the fate of peoples, was linked to a continuous ravelling and unravelling of wars, dynastic incidents and diplomatic exchanges whose protagonists were always a handful of more or less illustrious personages. An anecdote from the royal bedchamber could have unforeseen consequences. In such a context, clearly, the nasal dimension of a queen of Egypt suddenly acquires the most significant gravity.

41

Slowly but surely, however, criteria for judgment evolved and historians finally sorted out their viewpoint. This was determined, in general, by the advance of social sciences and basic, everyday evidence — of which we were becoming increasingly conscious — was brought to bear. A mere account of battles, palace intrigues and international treaties was no longer considered satisfactory: under closer inspection all this was indeed history, but certainly not the whole story. The weight of society, if I may so term it, remained on the sidelines. And everyday experience, analysis of modern reality certainly revealed that what was on the sidelines was precisely the fundamental issue. It was from this point that historians began to look more closely at these dark issues which make up the real fabric of social dynamics. Slowly but surely the idea flourished that it was this social dynamic — the formula we use to describe it is of secondary importance — which should be considered the basic material of historical study. Research has progressively made its components more apparent: economic anatomy, the ensuing class and group stratification, their corresponding antagonism, the segregating cultural and behavioural forms, the resulting means of production, and so many other factors. Wars and all the rest became no more than a gratuitous joke in bad taste, confabulated by certain glorious or ill-fated individuals and all were subsumed into that substratum of forces. And Cleopatra's nose — in other words, the personal ambition of some king, the idiocy or fanaticism of some clique, the impatience of conspirators and so forth — faded into the background. There came a moment when history could be written without proper names.

This type of historiographic sociology was limited at the start to individual interpretations. Such is the case with Marx. The erudite, meanwhile, continued as they were, chained to their own routine, but even they found themselves obliged to correct their perspective. Yet with one clear advantage: they could do without the apriorism which usually — and dangerously — deforms the vision of the interpreters. Today, monographic research dealing with one period in particular is more concerned with clarifying the results of a plague or a bad harvest, the movement of a port or the accounts of merchants than the intimacies of a chancellery or a palace. Perhaps this is not wholly the case: the intimacies of chancelleries and palaces have been bandied about enough and require no more airing. But the rest was ready to be investigated and that is what our researchers are continuing to do. When all is said and done it is only common sense. Nowadays, whenever we want to formulate an opinion about a country or a particular society we begin by examining its economic structure, the polarisation of its classes, the degree of antagonism between them, the mystifications which are superimposed. It is only when these key factors have been elucidated that we have the slightest possibility of understanding the incidences of its internal and foreign policies. The historian attempts something similar with the past. Objective and method are, to a certain extent, alike.

But what about Cleopatra's nose? The explanation for momentously superficial events — dynastic change, reversals of alliances, transition from one regime to another, civil war or international conflict — no longer lies in the whim of any monarch or individual in his marriage or adulteries, in factional unrest or patriotic hatred. Reasons of another kind will be adduced to explain them. Class confrontation, a conflict of business interests between rival groups of differing nationalities, monetary imbalance, demographic upsets; these will be the factors detected by the historian as agents of the mechanics of history. It is not always a case of independent phenomena, that is, phenomena rigorously independent of the will of these affected. It is also obvious that they are not a refraction of individual will. They are, rather, objective tendencies, both powerful and conditioning, which drag along in their wake the decisions of the protagonists. Kings, rulers, oligarchies are subject in history to impulses from a pressure-force exterior to themselves, although the direction of this force may coincide more often than not with their own best interest. Authentic power does not reside in the person who exercises it institutionally as much as from the real forces which hold up the institution and the person at the helm. Not even Cleopatra was simply the woman called Cleopatra; neither were Caesar and Mark Anthony simply her lovers. They all represented something more in a solemn political framework than their respective erotic longings.

That is the truth of the matter. But it is also beyond question that Cleopatra's nose — and both Caesar's and Mark Anthony's admiration for Cleopatra's nose — did have a certain bearing. Fate is impossible to eliminate. I refer to these fates which converge on these conspicuous characters whom traditional historiography places on the stage of the centuries. It is hardly worth considering the other fates. Voltaire ridiculed them in the *Dialogue d'un Brahmane et d'un Jésuite*. In this tale the patriarch of Ferney places in the mouth of a far and distant Hindu an amusing explanation of the death of Henry IV of France: the murder of the king would not have transpired had the Brahman in question not slipped one day on the banks of the Ganges. Unfortunately, in falling the oriental priest pushed into the river his Persian friend, Eribas, who drowned. The Persian's widow then married an Armenian trader and bore him a daughter who later married a Greek.

A daughter of this marriage settled in France and married the father of the regicide Ravaillac. Had the Brahman not slipped, Eriban would not have died, nor would his wife have married the Armenian *et cetera*, *et cetera*; nor would Ravaillac have been born, and so Henry IV would have died in his bed of pneumonia or diabetes like any decent person. Voltaire's humour was aimed at combating presumptuous concatenations about cause and effect which might seek to justify the development of history on the grand or small scale.

44

We can take their little tale in a wider sense. Ravaillac's dagger, and indeed Ravaillac himself, were not a *fate* from which the Hindu Brahman could have saved the French. On the other hand, the fate of being Cleopatra, of having a seductive nose, is not such a laughing matter. A Brahman's slip will never alter the chain of events: the slips and noses of powerful individuals, though not altering it, at least condition it in their own way.

Let us take Napoleon. It is quite probable given the circumstances that the Revolution would inevitably end up with a dictatorship; Bonapartism might well have become prominent due to the profound demands made on the social coagulations of France at that time. Somebody had to be the dictator: fate decreed it be Napoleon. If Bonapartism was a trick of fate, Bonaparte himself was in no way *fated*: the strong man of Bonapartism could well have been someone else. And we are quite within our rights to suppose that this self-same historical conflagration would have been, had power been assumed by a different person, if not of a different nature, at least of a distinct influence. To spend time imagining what would have become of Europe in the first part of the nineteenth century if Napoleon's shoes had been worn by someone else would be, I admit, useless and untimely entertainment. Nonetheless, such hypotheses are difficult to avoid when we start to ponder the ups and downs of history. I feel not the slightest sympathy for the figure of Bonaparte; at the same time no one could deny his exceptional gifts as a politician, strategist and adventurer. The consequences of his march across the continent — from Madrid to Moscow, from Naples to Berlin — are binding. The spread of liberal ideology that accompanied his armies and the nationalist reactions that the great Corsican aroused are the basis of Modern Europe. All this, and more, that we credit to Napoleon's account would have happened even without Napoleon: let us have no doubts about it. But who is there that would argue that it would have been realised in the same fashion and with the same rapidity? A First Consul not stirred by ambition, without military know-how or diplomatic energy, mediocre — a bonaparte with a small b — would have taken certain aspects of French policy in another direction and would have reduced the virulence of other points. Napoleon was yet a further Cleopatra's nose.

The truth of the matter is that, as long as there remains the possibility for one person, or a group of people, to retain an exceptional and decisive amount of power in their hands, there will always be a Cleopatra's nose lying in wait. Leafing through today's papers we can see that this is still the case. Take the present Fifth Republic in France. What would it have been, what could it be, what will it be, without General de Gaulle? Isn't the perdurance of any autocratic regime totally linked to the physical and mental health of the autocrat? Doesn't the Stalin affair, in the version given by the leaders of the Soviet Union today, reveal that the objective laws which govern the house of socialism have been on the point of suffering a serious and unpredictable setback thanks to the Georgian dictator's intemperate gorging?

Isn't it mere fate that the Fifth French Republic should be as it is — its fate being that its highest position of power has ended up in the hands of de Gaulle, a prestigious, highly decorated megalomaniac? Is it not fate that certain countries are the subject of praetorian systems? Fate decrees it should be this and not some other despot whose life, when medically assured, maintains the official foundation. It was no act of fate that the Soviet Union became a monolithic state with an absolute hierarchy and controlled by secret police. Fate merely dictated that supreme power centred on a man like Stalin: unbalanced, paranoid and vengeful. History proceeds along its course in line with the game of the infernal forces which propel it; but on occasions and precisely at the most delicate moment there's a Cleopatra's nose that steps in. The influence of fate will be of a greater or lesser degree according to the particular case. At times it will be favourable, at others, harmful. I don't propose to evaluate this or that here. My intention is merely to point out this fact.

Quite clearly, Cleopatra's noses are not the only faces worthy of mention. In an under-developed society, for example, which depends fundamentally on an agrarian economy, years of continuous drought or dreadful rainfall can mean a total collapse with unforeseeable social and political ramifications. A decisive war, lost or won through some eventual military or technical turnabout, can change many things; for example, If Hitler had had the atomic bomb...? It would be very simple to multiply the fateful probabilities of indisputable transcendence. But for all this, it is Cleopatra's nose which remains the most disturbing thing. Fate here becomes incarnate in one person, or in a handful of people. And so long as societies are so structured that a single individual, or a handful of individuals, retain power in all its fullness, this will be inevitable. The all-powerful governor is a man or woman, not a machine to govern; their omnipotence will never escape a personal use. Perhaps it's idealistic to hope that one day humanity will free itself from this type of risk. For the moment, only a form of public government has managed to reduce to the minimum the probable impertinence of any Cleopatra with an admirable nose — the same form which has reduced to a minimum the authoritative faculties of governors. The future, however, does not seem too well disposed to such a state. If tomorrow technocrats are to be in charge, as the sociologists predict, and if their power is also to be final and all-ensuing, Cleopatra's-nose-syndrome will continue to be a threat to the sweet, colourless and resigned mass of subjects whose only aspiration is to live this life in peace and in God's grace.

FATUOUSNESS

What would become of our lives, of our everyday mediocre existence, if we couldn't allow ourselves the luxury of vanity? The human being is a fatuous animal — the only one on the zoological ladder with such a capacity. Everything we do is prompted by vanity. Insofar as ambition itself has a recognisable purpose it is not power or wealth, fame or respect, but just enough power, wealth, fame and respect to justify our conceit. Everyone, in his own ambit and so far as his ability permits, is seeking this: vanity satisfied. There are even some who use humility to achieve it. What counts is to be important: important at the office, the academy, with one's neighbours, in the gossip columns, in people's chit-chat.

This is the great means that humanity, the individual and perhaps the individualist have discovered for passing the time pleasantly. Time or, if you prefer, life. It's all one and the same thing.

FLÂNER

A neighbour of mine, a talkative, well-read shopkeeper who in his youth spent several years living in Paris, has given me a book by Bernanos in an unusual edition. The book is a reminder of those happy days he spent in Paris. We talk about them.

"I'd promised myself two things and I kept my promise to the letter: never to pawn any item I owned and never to borrow a centime from anyone... Paris is a wonderful city but an expensive one. I mean the nice side of Paris, the theatres and concerts, the opera and the cabaret. At least it was in my day."

"I can't think things have changed much..."

"I was earning a paltry sum. And what can a young foreigner get up to in Paris without money in his pocket?"

I think up an impartial, moral, evasive reply.

"Walk round..."

"That's right. Not really walking round: *flâner*. Some words you can't translate. *Flâner* in French, how would you translate it? *Flâner* is walking round, roaming the streets, that's true. But I feel it's something else besides."

"Absolutely."

"*Flâner* is a wonderful pastime. We'd finish work in the

afternoon and not know what to do. The most economical solution was to go for a walk. To wander around aimlessly, peacefully, without preconceptions. It was most enjoyable."

"I imagine so."

"*Flâner* is to walk around but to do so in a special way. People here don't walk around like they do there."

"Probably not. Here we'd rather not walk, or if we do, it's to admire the scenery, or to carry on the conversation we struck up with our pals at the club, or to get the sun on our faces."

"My experience has led me to the conclusion that *flâner* is a creation peculiar to the folklore of Paris. Only the setting of Paris makes something like that possible."

He pauses and I wait for him to go on.

"The streets, the people you came across as you walked along... they didn't interest you at all. They were streets just like any other street and the people were strangers. And yet looking at them and wondering at them kept you entertained. You forgot them immediately afterwards. But while it lasted it was enjoyable."

"The world really is a funny old spectacle."

"The world? Paris."

All this may be just the leftovers of a literary intoxication lying within my friend's memory. I don't know. Neither can I say whether the semantic value he attached to the verb *flâner*, based on the recollections of his youth, has any value.

"*Flâner*...", he repeats, still wrapped up in his memories. I think of Bernanos and can't picture him in Paris. But it doesn't really matter.

FREEDOM

It might be a bit over the top, a joke almost, to put forward the notion of the music of spheres. Pythagoras's venerable opinion wouldn't command much respect nowadays, not even as a metaphysical reference. But in the same way that, according to that illustrious philosopher of antiquity, we humans are unaware of the more or less melodious sound — sound — given off by the workings of the universe, so there are those who maintain that people living near Niagara Falls don't hear the non-stop thundering of the waters of those famous cascades. The reason for both instances of insensitivity towards sound must be the same: the fact of being used to the noise in question to such an extent that it is no longer perceived. The spheres that made up the cosmos, according to the gratifying explanation furnished by the Greek sage, had been revolving forever, endlessly; our eardrums receive their music naturally, he suggests, but we cannot discern it because we're familiar with it from the very moment we're born. A similar familiarity affects the hearing of those residing in the environs of the famous geological accident of Niagara — I believe this quite sincerely. More down-to-earth experiences confirm this possibility: people who handle noisy machinery get used to its continual racket, and the din — which for anyone else would be an annoying and dangerous noise — for them is just a practically unimportant background hum. You can extend this practically as much as you please; the remark is still valid. And if this is the case among people subjected to ear-splitting sources during work hours only, what must it be like for those who put up with such things for twenty-four hours a day for years on end?

Whatever the truth of the matter, these reflections, vague and frivolous as they are, seek to draw attention to a phenomenon which both goes beyond and encompasses them. I am thinking of the enervating power of many kinds of familiarity which are imposed on us or which we accept and which affect countless aspects of our everyday lives. On a more or less personal plane we have our routines: the petty, meaningless routines, domestic and banal, which centre on the most humdrum form of jogging along. Weighed down by those, we fail to see how they condition or complicate the naturalness of our behaviour. Many routines, through the fact of being just that, become real taboos for us, simultaneously inhibiting and coercing us. More or less the same thing happens in the field of social relationships and their public equivalents. Here certain familiarities, those that last and take root with penetrating omnipotence — not an unusual occurrence — eventually blunt our senses: our civil senses, if I can use such a phrase. The particular deafness which would stop us hearing the music of the spheres or which prevents the natives of Niagara from hearing the crashing waterfall, recurs and takes over in each and every one of us where usualness is concerned. In practice we're deaf to everything that's come to be a burdensome, tedious habit. We run the permanent risk of falling into a paralysing error: mistaking the habitual for the normal and taking this normality as good and virtuous on some occasions, and certain and inviolable on others. This much is obvious.

We might illustrate this, by way of an example, with the problem of freedom. Or, to be more accurate, with two problems: freedom and the lack of freedom, since both are equally usual in the world today. People accustomed to living in an atmosphere where subjection and orders from above are the norm may become deaf — deaf to the lack of freedom surrounding and oppressing them. Those who, by contrast, are accustomed to the luxuries of choice and ease may also be deaf to the advantages of their state. The former, stupefied by tyranny, are probably not even capable of gauging the violence of the mutilation inflicted upon their dignity: the latter, trusting in the presumed guarantees of the law, probably forget the responsibility and precariousness of their blessing — the blessing of freedom. These two perils often nibble away at or poison the roots of individuals'conduct, regardless of the political regime in force. Habit acquires an insidious, anaesthetic effect. This means that unless they put up a clear-thinking, watchful resistance, citizens are condemned to a fate of semi-blind passivity. Most subjects of a dictatorship, accustomed to it, don't regret their lost freedom; most subjects of a law-abiding state — in theory the proper climate for freedom

— accustomed to this, fail to appreciate the immunity it provides. Both sorts of deafness lead to what is merely familiar being regarded as natural — fair, irrevocable, rigid.

Familiarity and familiarisation, in this case as in so many others, merely dumbfound and depress. Their effects are fleeting or expendable — usually, at any rate. The deafness they lead to is not genuine. However, the disease can become chronic, aggravated by its own persistence. Those workers who handle noisy pieces of machinery, partially immunised against the background noise, can eventually become genuinely deaf: their ears finally give in. If our deafness to freedom, or the lack of it, is chronic, it can lay us open to irreversible deformity. Habit, which for the moment simply benumbs us, in the long term substantially undermines our best moral defences. From being artificially deaf we become genuinely deaf. The transition may not be very spectacular and the person undergoing it will refuse to accept and acknowledge it. But atrophy, however we choose to term it, occurs. This is why there are so many people deaf to the lack of freedom, who hide themselves away in submissiveness and patient inertia: resigned to it, they'll never be able to escape and, what is worse, they will sometimes not even want to. This is also why there are so many people deaf to freedom, the freedom they enjoy, who are defenceless and bewildered when under threat or attack. The similarity with physically deaf people is not absolute in the final analysis. Physically deaf people know they are disabled and regard their handicap as just that, a shortcoming: whereas the other kind of deaf people have no idea of their deafness. This lack of awareness is an additional factor making the situation worse.

We needn't over-insist on the moral to be inferred from the preceding remarks. It is sufficient that, from time to time, some Pythagoras should come along to remind us that the spheres have their music; it is sufficient that someone goes up to the natives of Niagara to tell them —

in case they doubt it — that their Falls make an over-whelming noise. To put it another way: it is sufficient that, in the face of our own habits — our familiarity, be it spontaneous or forced — we ourselves realise that they are only customs, only habits. Only in this way can we escape from the sleep-inducing suggestiveness stemming from them. We must always bear in mind that the reverse possibility will help us appreciate the precise extent of our auditory health.

For even if Pythagoras's spheres don't exist — or their music — even if the whole tale of the residents of Niagara is a lie, the truth regarding social deafness is indisputable. It's worth thinking about.

HELL

In Aldous Huxley I read the phrase posthumous revenge.
Huxley is referring, of course, to what, in our vocabulary
based on the catechism, we call hell. Posthumous revenge,
quite so: isn't this a clear, straightforward, exact way of
defining the idea of hell as it is professed by most of those
who believe in it? Basically it's all a question of hope. Just
as there exists one kind of unnecessary hope which allows
us to envisage eternal salvation, there is another which
relates to eternal damnation. Needless to say, I'm being
precise here in my choice of terms. This latter type of hope
is, however, only thought of as a prospect which may affect
our neighbour, our fellow creature. No one, unless they
are a perverted monster in questions of eternity, will dare
to hope that they will suffer the gloomy discomforts of
hell. For this too is taken for granted: that hell is a place,
assuming the word place is acceptable, of enormous and
never-ending suffering, a state of permanent pain, of punishment par excellence, categorical and harsh. Naturally
enough, we fear hell for ourselves. But we wish it on other
people: we always wish it on someone else.

Such a wish is reassuring. We ought not to feel ashamed
to confess it. Life is organised in such a way that actually
a lot of what we see and dub unfair, in terms both of
things and people, has no possible redress in the course of
our ephemeral lives. The tyrant, the usurer, the
hypocrite, the murderer, the impertinent, the libertine
and so many others, rarely if ever receive a punishment in
keeping with their crimes. I am still using the terminology appropriate to the subject. In their thoughts, words
and deeds, tyrants, usurers, hypocrites, murderers,
impertinents and libertines subject us to outrage, a great

deal of outrage: specifically against any one of us and in general against the hypothetical order of the world. Often, all too often, they escape the punishment they merit in all honesty. Sometimes they escape it because they're powerful, other times because they're clever or adroit; justice — this is quite clear — is not done in this vale of tears. We like to imagine another life, albeit just for this reason: another life where an absolute, all-powerful decision, scrupulously fair, would re-establish the normality of the *suum quique*.

It's an appealing idea: punishment *post mortem*, applied in keeping with a yardstick both unbending and precise. Let's call this hell. Hell becomes necessary if we want the universe not to be absurd. And, in the final analysis, this desire, this hope is no more than an expression of revenge: we transfer to God, the Judge, our justified wish of reprisal. Posthumous revenge. Those who have consulted them say that the mediaeval scholastics — none more so than Thomas Aquinas — held that one of the delights of heavenly bliss will lie in enjoying the spectacle of evildoers in hell. Peacefully settled into paradise, the virtuous ectoplasms will not be satisfied wish the blessed vision or contemplation of God: they will also need an extra source of contentment consisting of the joy at verifying that the wicked do actually burn in the relentless fires, endlessly poked at and tortured by devils. It must be said that this statement, or assertion, makes good sense.

I used the word joy on purpose. At the heart of all revenge there is a core of joy which I cannot bring myself to criticise. Aren't those who have suffered down here entitled to compensation up there? They are, moreover, entitled to compensation at the expense of the particular individual they hold guilty of their earthly misfortunes. On a higher plane, almost a political one, Dante is a perfect example of all this. The first part of his *Commedia* — the *Inferno* — could be spoken of as a great epic of revenge: of posthumous revenge. The acrimonious Florentine creates a hell of prodigious decasyllables and places therein precisely all the characters who were the object of his pet hates. Dante's readers take it for granted that the opinion — the judgment of the poet may have nothing to do with any probable opinion or judgment of God's. And neither did Dante uphold any such identification. Wouldn't it have been idiotic and fatuous of him to subject himself to the judgment of the Deity and hand out sentences in free and easy fashion? But when Dante invents his *inferno* he is simply giving free rein to an abundant vein of revenge. No doubt once he had written those lines he felt more relaxed and free. Of course not everyone is a Dante, nor does everyone have sufficient time and imagination to think up a hell to work out his own grudges. And then we think of that other hell, a real hell not a literary one, with dreadful torments and lasting forever. It's our own small, obstinate, insatiable revenge. A posthumous one.

HUMILIATION
We all feel humiliated by different things. For instance, I know people who feel a cosmic sense of outrage because their bodies in no way resemble a Greek statue.

IDEAS

Any coincidence between my ideas and yours is just that: pure coincidence.

INDIGNATION

We sometimes seem to think that indignation is just another category, like so many others, of wrath. An indignant person, however little he flies off the handle, always looks as though he had surrendered to the impulse of fury. In all honesty it would be rash to claim this is not the case. All indignation implies, to one degree or another, is a burst of exasperation directed against something or someone: against that which causes indignation. The consensus of dictionaries tends to list this fury among the varieties of wrath. All right then: a theologian, a moralist, might assuage our fears, assuring us that the wrath in question does not lie within the jurisdictional bounds of the well-known deadly sin. Apparently, approached from different angles, there are wraths and wraths: some reproachable and others with a veneer of decorum. Did not the people of Israel, a touchstone for so many attitudes, conceive of their Jehovah as a wrathful divinity, or at least with tendencies in that direction? And, unless I'm mistaken, St Thomas Aquinas also drew distinctions regarding the essence of anger.

If indignation is a form of wrath, at least it isn't simply another category, one among many. Quite the reverse, it is the form of anger proper to virtue. Indignation and virtue are, ultimately correlative commodities. And so, when confronted with formulae such as the God of wrath or the wrath of God which our modern religious vocabulary has inherited from the Jews, sensitive souls should prefer the

57

use of the word indignation instead of wrath: the God of indignation, the indignation of God. This is not merely because the word wrath is overladen with centuries-old negative connotations. There is another reason: the semantic roots of the word indignation — I'm no expert in etymology, but I venture to guess this is right — contain a shred of indicative evidence. Indignation, in fact, takes for granted the dignity of those who experience it and the indignity of their victim. The virtuous party is always the one to become indignant; the one to suffer the outbursts of indignation is always the wicked party.

Virtue, precisely because of its dignity, becomes indignant. An indignant man may be evil or frivolous: but insofar as he becomes indignant he does so out of a virtuous conviction — virtuous in his own eyes — which he maintains unshaken. In reality everyone becomes indignant at one time or another since everyone, in his own way, has this kind of conviction. In order to protect oneself from the danger of feeling indignation one should be completely lacking in dignity and this, acknowledging oneself to be totally unworthy, is beyond our capabilities. When one becomes indignant, one is merely reacting to the indignity of others: an irrepressible urge stoked up by solid and shadowy justifications. It would be extremely revealing to draw up an analytical catalogue of the types of indignation prevalent in a period or place, in a specific society: it would provide us with a detailed illustration of the moral tenets on which people's lives are based. A moral code is seen far more vigorously and actively in the indignation which feeds it than in the exemplary behaviour expressing or repressing it.

Because it's an odd thing in practice, men forget when they become indignant that they themselves might also be the object of indignation. It is not unusual for a depraved individual to feel indignant at the depravity of his neighbour. Let he who is without sin cast the first stone is one of the least respected Christian teachings. Hypocrisy? Perhaps in part, but not entirely. Indignation is aroused on a

58

different level from hypocrisy. We're hypocritical when our personal well-being is at stake, for that very reason. Whereas we become indignant even when, at times because, we have nothing to do with the cause thereof. The sinner most aware of his own sins is indignant at the sins of others, and quite rightly so. Rightly, since he is indignant in the name of virtue. What he (the sinner!) finds offensive is seeing virtue trampled on: that same virtue, or maybe another, he himself has trampled on. Of course he could, and should, have started by feeling indignant with himself: but whether he does or not, the other person is objectively provoking the indignation he has every right to feel.

What remains to be investigated is whether virtue needs indignation or not in order to carry on being virtue: I mean in order to confirm itself as such in men's minds. Probably. But this problem lies beyond my capacity to comment. It is best left to the experts in the field.

INTELLECTUAL

What remains of Erasmus today? Merely his name. Or practically so. A couple of his writings may occasionally be read. The fact that both Latin and Christianity have fallen into disuse means that Erasmus's work, rooted in the living usage of the one and the efficacy of the other, has also sunk into oblivion. Present-day readers, if they are curious and have nothing more pressing to hand, will manage the *Praise of Folly* fairly effortlessly and may even enjoy it, since satire, even when targeting ghosts, is always entertaining. It wouldn't be entirely pointless to leaf through the spirited *Querela pacis* occasionally, particularly now, in an age with a leaning towards martial excitability, since we might find therein — as in some of the minor works, similarly disregarded over the years, of our own Vives — a venerable, well-reasoned lesson. I can't tell, though, whether the *Enchiridion* could retain our attention: it doesn't mine, at least. For people such as myself, a mere unscholarly passer-by, the titles and subject-matter alone of the other books by Erasmus — biblical and patristic glosses and translations, his correspondence and polemical papers — would suffice to put us off, to discourage us from reading them. In spite of all this, Erasmus's name lives on and does so with a half-glorious certainty. It isn't merely his own fame and simple inertia which tends to keep alive in the memory of generations a prestige once vibrant but now eclipsed; there's something else: an enduring, immediate, living reputation as an example. Erasmus the man, the intellectual attitude he made one with his life, is what we still admire in him. Among the lay saints of today's world, the humanist of Rotterdam occupies a special place and receives the devotion, be it hasty or otherwise, of his professional colleagues in the twentieth century: I refer to those intellectuals who, not being entirely committed to a party or church, keep for themselves, with a few misgivings, the title of liberals.

A primary reason why Erasmus is a real brother in destiny for us is the very drama of his activity as a writer. In another age more peaceful or solid than ours this would undoubtedly have been less obvious. The intellectual has not always been faced with a pressing need to choose, to opt for one of the warring factions that divide society. In this respect the early sixteenth century resembled our own age. Erasmus was confronted with a moment of revolution — in his day, a religious revolution — like the intellectual of today with a social revolution and in both cases the very fact of the revolution and its consequences, foreign in some measure to the way the writer might approach them, was thrust upon them forcefully. Both Rome and Luther demanded of Erasmus that he come out clearly in favour of their stance, naturally, and Erasmus knew that his conscience was dictating fondness and animosity towards each of the combatants, simultaneously and partially. If he saw in the rebellious monk a purifying hope, at the same time he saw in the Church of Rome the institutional guarantee of Christianity. Erasmus neither wavered nor felt restrained: he wanted to conciliate, which is quite a different matter; he sought a synthesis which would combine the positive values — positive in his eyes — belonging to each of the contenders. With the recent rise of engagement as a watchword, the moral status of most of our contemporary writers has become analogous to some extent with that of Erasmus. Today's intellectuals, invited or threatened by the warring factions or the interests or pressures at stake, are reliving Erasmus's adventure leaving aside, as is only natural, the differences in character and circumstance.

It is only to be expected that some friction should be produced, particularly once a certain point is reached: when what was for the intellectual a simple question of ideas or conduct becomes the substance and moving force behind collective readjustments. In general, a theoretical proposition may always be transformed into the reason behind social upheaval, if such be its sense as regards the established *status quo*. But, looked at objectively, the possibility for danger varies depending on the nature of the surroundings in which it occurs. A philosophy such as Erasmus's *Philosophia*, had it appeared 200 years earlier or later, would have been inoffensive or, at any rate, more inoffensive: it might have passed unnoticed; no one would have cared about it with such rigour and anxiety. In the early sixteenth century, however, it was bound to assume an inflammatory function and inflammatory proportions. The high standing of the man and the appeal of his doctrine could be important factors within that religious upheaval: they could exert a huge influence on the debate in progress between orthodoxy and reform. They all wanted Erasmus to align himself, unconditionally, with their side since in winning Erasmus they won the valuable support of intellectual authority, a sagacious colleague and the select band of his admirers scattered throughout Europe. Erasmus took fright when he glimpsed the prospect lying before him — *precisely* before him. In his temporary lodgings as a humanist, a nomadic man of letters, he wrote and wrote because writing was his job, his mission; but in the world outside, two opposing armies latched onto his wonderful writings as if they were documents of support or sabotage; at least they were prepared to take them, to consider them, in this light.

The stance of Erasmus of Rotterdam was untenable, though. The warring factions then, as now, must be *absolute*, exclusive and total incarnations of the truth as regards both theory and practice. Joining one of them, therefore, implied subjection. And this is what Erasmus refused to do. He would side with neither party since he had his objections to both. At times, his own personal beliefs coincided in part with those of the Germanic rebels and at other times in part with the traditional standpoint of Rome. Further, he was to remain faithful to this personal conviction and to none other. But this was what the others, the combatants, failed to comprehend: they saw the religious issue of the moment only in terms of a cut and dried formula, he who is not with me is against me, translated into the practical vocabulary of politics. This led, inevitably, to the humanist being regarded as suspect by both parties: suspected of playing the enemy's game. And the fact is that they were both correct in their suspicions. Erasmus was neither a declared enemy nor neutral (an enemy too ashamed to say so); he was something worse, a treacherous ally. For the Roman Catholic church he was still a member — he never left it formally — only with a dash of heresy; for the Lutherans, a kindred spirit, often a master, an inspiration, yet incapable of breaking with obedience to the Pope.

Things became more complicated for Erasmus when he wanted, and needed, to accommodate this obstinate design of his — on which rested his independence — with his personal problems which still arose from proclaiming and practising that ambition. Alas! Erasmus needed to eat and more often than not he had to eat at the expense of kings and religious or secular lords who paid him a stipend or allowance. Erasmus's benefactors were, quite naturally, directly concerned, involved, in the religious feud. Not only must the humanist avoid the snares and persecution threatening him from all quarters, he must also retain a minimum of material peace and quiet to enable him to carry on working. As he sought to hang on to the support of the powerful classes and to provide himself with a relatively secure refuge Erasmus was obliged to walk a tightrope, apparent maybe, but never-ending and perilous: he tried to maintain this position, which forced upon him a continuous attitude of self-defence, of unending excuses in the face of accusations which laid him open to losing his benefits. The story of his dealings with the Catholic sector is very revealing. Branded as a heretic by hair-splitting, fierce theologians, Erasmus never tired of writing justifications to prove his orthodoxy. At the same time, he did eventually join in the anti-Lutheran campaign. It seems as if the writer yields repeatedly either to external pressures or to his own fears rather than to any desire to express things more specifically. He would doubtless have preferred to apply himself to writing a major work, instead of replying to self-centred monks, as he would also have chosen to remain silent rather than join in the anti-Lutheran chorus. But he had to do both of these out of what he deemed expediency. We must remember, though, that when Erasmus was thus put on the spot, he was not insincere. Had he gone for pretence, he could have adopted the militant stance the Catholics demanded of him, thereby thwarting the suspicions of the religious community and the Curia. He was repelled by show and servility. So, despite everything, he basically stood his ground: he knew suspicion would not fade away simply because he wrote books attacking Luther; he wrote them, though, just in the hope that his enemies' anger would be toned down and, in passing, that he would retain the indulgence of his pro-Rome protectors.

The state of the present-day intellectual is no longer that of Erasmus's time. Faced with the contemporary conflict, the educated person, at least in the western world, is in a somewhat similar situation. However, he is no longer dependent on the largesse of benefactors who must be kept happy, nor is he so vulnerable to inquisitorial repression. The financial subjugation of the writer to a particular class — the dominant class, which buys his books and flatters him — still persists to a certain extent and there are still coercive procedures, open, or otherwise, that hold back his activities for the benefit of that same class (which, needless to say, constitutes one of the warring factions in our present battle). But although the risks he runs are neither as many nor as great as those facing the sixteenth-century humanist, he still fears them. The symbolic power exercised nowadays by the figure of Erasmus stems from the fact that, like him, our contemporary intellectuals reject the servility implicit in any commitment and, also like him, lack the bravery, the courage, to stand up to the harshness of an unfriendly society. The western writer is frightened to commit himself utterly to a more or less unofficial communism, since he realises he might be thought of as functional; he is frightened, moreover, of breaking all his ties with the middle-class machinery he opposes but which, when it comes down to it, protects and feeds him. He himself is, to put it one way, in opposition: above all, in deepest opposition (or maybe contradiction) to the established order. A good number of our men of letters — those who have inspired these thoughts — are offended if one brings up their middle-class connections; even when they don't dare deny them, they do their best to make an exception, to absolve themselves from the sinister responsibilities resting on capitalist society. They do take trouble, though, as did Erasmus, not to be associated with the *other* opposition, the real, militant opposition, that of the revolutionary party, regardless of all possible coincidences. At the same time they take trouble to hang on to those advantages which the bourgeois world assigns them, without this leading them to renounce their position as antagonists, which they still proclaim, albeit cautiously. The precarious tightrope on which Erasmus sought to stand upright is now reproduced on a large scale and under a disturbing variety of guises.

It would, however, be a mistake, and unfair, to believe that the problem being aired is merely one of well-being, of comfortable safeguard. In fact this is not even the main problem. I've chosen to draw attention to it in the first place, to highlight it, only so as to clear the issue in advance of all foreseeable emphasis. The reason is obvious. It's well-known that the intellectual tends to surround his ministrations with an almost religious air; actually this is far from gratuitous since, when all is said and done, his rôle in society replaces certain functions of the old, decrepit teachings of the priests or the occasional attempt at prophecy: guidance and deterrent. But it is also true that he is not unaffected by the troubles which assail any other kind of man: passions and individual weaknesses, incentives and social interests. Logically, the intellectual tends to conceal this latter aspect through sheer decency. It was important, though, to stress the relevance of the factor to which I was referring before proceeding any further. It was important to state openly that Erasmus was no hero and to suggest, in passing, that heroism is a talent unknown to the literary family. Among men of letters we will never come across a hero. There have been rogues, and there still are — like Villon, Juan Ruiz or Jean Genet; spoiled aristocrats — like Goethe, Ausiàs March or Shelley; madmen — like Llull or Léon Bloy; cowards or drudges — like the majority. Neither the stylish sort, such as Rimbaud, nor the countless suicides, not even those who starve themselves to death have anything to do with heroism, the heroism to which I am referring here. For I am referring particularly to the unbending resistance the literary person should put up against the devious or menacing requirements of society so as to maintain and advocate, without concessions, both his doctrinal viewpoints and inherent opinions *as well as the right he has to do so*, all of this regardless of cost and with the strictest ethical and psychological cohesiveness. Erasmus wasn't a hero of that ilk. Neither are any of the intellectuals who are today playing out his drama. So I ought, maybe, to correct what I wrote at the beginning: let us say now, rather, that the significance of Erasmus is not exemplary but merely representative. If we are, just a little, admirers of his — of his life history, I repeat, not his books — this is because it is always comforting to think that someone has existed in whom we recognise the image of our own concerns and our own bewilderment endured for once with the maximum dignity possible.

I was saying, though, that it wasn't all a problem of ease. In the give-and-take of subterfuge and excuses indulged in by the humanist of Rotterdam we can immediately appreciate more motives than the simple aim of earning a derisory income or sparing himself difficulties with the powers watching over him. Erasmus mistrusted the parties in conflict and he did so out of what was the innermost core of his belief. His enemies on either side, by attacking him, not only attacked a particular ideological stance — his seemingly ambiguous *philosophia Christi*. They were also attacking *belles lettres* or, to put it in modern parlance, culture. Erasmus considered himself one of the undoubted mainstays of restored humanism, *litterae humaniores*, and no one dared, or will ever dare, to disagree. He is also certain that reborn *belles lettres* are valuable in themselves, one of the highest values that mankind could pride itself on at that time. The barbarism of Luther and of the monks equally places the advances of humanism in peril, being a return to servile, ignorant medievalism. Neither is the climate of violence through which Europe is living conducive to this new literary statement, or at least his ideas of expansive continuity. Barbarism and violence, the one engenders the other. And the exact word that needs to be mentioned here is, without doubt, freedom. The present-day intellectual has never ceased thinking of it. Erasmus was aware of the fierce sectarianism which was the order of the day, lying in wait for him: suspicious on the one hand of the restless search for perfection, which is an essential part of the creative task of the meticulous, demanding writer, of the humanist aspiring to elegance of form and content; and on the other seeking to turn the man of letters into a propagandist, an apostle of their sect, to reduce him to its dogmatism, its conventions. Erasmus knew that if either of the warring factions triumphed all that he had pressed for and protected would be destroyed: humanism, in a word his humanism, which had introduced these two new factors, namely, enjoyment derived from detailed, subtle work and freedom from the imposed fetters of doctrine. The intellectual of today has the same fears.

Violence still exists: both in actual events and that which springs from tense, difficult moments when issues of intellectual debate are also the issues leading to large-scale clashes. And barbarism still exists in one guise or another. For the sixteenth-century humanist, as for the twentieth-century writer of the western world, barbarism is whatever imperils the set of conditions within which intellectual processes occur *as they understand them*: in short, conditions of freedom. However much he may be in agreement with those in revolt, the man of letters is unwilling to join them: were he to do so, he would be turning his back on that freedom and becoming a mere mouthpiece of the decreed doctrine and a scholarly servant in their campaigns. Erasmus, far more than Luther, is the representative of a genuine free examination in the sense this phrase has in the secular field of intelligence. Modern European culture has virtually inherited it from Erasmus and made it the centre of intellectual awareness. Only when his freedom, inner and outer, is vouchsafed does the man of letters believe himself capable of carrying on in this rôle. This freedom, moreover, backs up his professional achievement.

We are, however, far removed from any aestheticist affectation. If the writer is attempting to withdraw from any confessional discipline this is not because he is feigning ignorance of the burning questions or because he sees his art as an end in itself, superior to society's other goals. Erasmus certainly repudiated the bad Latin of his enemies but also their bad scholasticism: good Latin and concomitant good scholasticism were practised by Erasmus. He was not playing at being a Ciceronian orator. His love of style, relentless correction, elegance of expression — these were never an end in themselves for him; neither, perhaps, a means — he regarded them as inseparable from the ideological content they express. Here, as always, it is not wise to make distinctions: it all rests on a single and profound initial resolution. The Christianity preached by Erasmus is the religious manifestation of an attitude which also appears in a specific fashion in literature. The attacks on the former also affect the latter, and vice versa. A modern parallel is not hard to find. When intellectuals refuse to commit themselves, to enlist, this is not in order to shirk their responsibilities and lock themselves up in a supposed ivory tower of Art for Art's sake. Some do seek this way out, but they are not the ones I'm talking of here. Today's man of letters is no stranger to the crucial issues of his work nor does he want to be: he has his views on them, he shares in them and has whatever influence he's allowed on them. And, in reality, his literature is not created in isolation from the conclusions he has reached in this area. Literature and — forgive me the limitations of my vocabulary — opinion form a single unquestionable entity in his eyes. The freedom he guards so jealously is a basic necessity for him; without it there's no chance of taking on responsibility when faced with problems. There's no chance of literature. In his mind, culture must compulsorily be rooted in those conditions laid down, more in theory than in fact, by liberal society.

This may be no more than a prejudice or an opinion distorted by the petit-bourgeois nature of the mentality prevalent among our western writers. The testimony of history could confirm that there have been periods, long ones, when culture, as respectable a culture as our own, has been viable under very different conditions: under conditions radically other than liberal. Naturally, intellectuals' concerns are today focused on the dogmatic, absolutist aspirations of communism. Thierry Maulnier — a right-wing writer, consequently in no way suspect — did not rule out the possibility of a communist Bossuet. We must admit that, in the realm of supposition, not only a Bossuet but even a Dante is possible. Actually Dante could be one of the geniuses who might be cited in favour of an illiberal culture since the Middle Ages, so strong on orthodoxy and hierarchical structure, *allowed* him. So, freedom — liberal freedom — is unnecessary either for genius or for the writer who doesn't quite make it that far. However, we must first remember that it is necessary for a particular sort of genius or writer; and secondly, that it is precisely this sort of genius or writer that intellectuals today, because he is theirs, wish to safeguard against communism and anti-communism. The memory of Erasmus comes back to mind. The culture we have defined as liberal has its source in him. The humanist of Rotterdam initiated a period in the moral life of the western world, distinguished by its break with the concept which had lasted throughout the Middle Ages of an ecclesiastical or paraecclesiastical culture, subordinate and adjacent. For all his cunning, despite all his concessions, Erasmus was writing outside the Church of Rome and was staying equally distant from Lutheranism. From that period on, the European man of letters was to seek to preserve his autonomy and to widen it thus confronting the powers-that-be, injustice and intimidation. Maybe this aim has become a little petulant over the years. But from a psychological angle this is a factor of some importance. For so long as this conviction is held deeply by the modern intellectual, he will never abandon his reserve. For better or worse. Cowardly, cheating, he will attempt to resist. As did Erasmus, the poor, sick, weak, cautious, reticent, wily, ambiguous Erasmus of Rotterdam...

INTEREST

A friend surprises me engrossed in reading a heavy medieval tome. Amazed, he asks, "Are you really interested in this?" He says "really" with a touch of incredulity.

I'm dismayed at his undoubted good faith. He reads another kind of material: in any case, he'd never be interested in a boring archaic text. I say boring because it would be for him and nearly everyone else. Is it for me? I must admit it isn't. I'm interested in it.

"Yes, I am."

What does interest mean? "A sentiment aroused in us by something, causing us to pay special attention to it, to be favourable or unfavourable towards it." I copy this out word for word from the Fabra Dictionary. As always, this dictionary turns up trumps: it's concise; complete, exact. That's all right, then. I'm interested in this ancient, dense book which deals with problems long dead and is written with abstruse, or crumbling, rhetoric.

"And why are you interested in it?"

To tell the truth, I've no idea what to say now. Maybe I should bring out my whole life history. My intellectual preferences and my occupation have for many years brought me into contact with unpolished anachronistic texts, treatises written by monks and friars, metaphysical poems diametrically opposed to my own way of seeing the world. But I can't dodge the question.

I improvise a reply on the spot.

"You only need to study something, the most trivial thing, for five minutes to get interested in it."

This phrase comes, dressed up in different words, from any one of the French moralists. The French — the moralists — have thought out excuses for every situation: Montaigne, La Rochefoucauld, Pascal, Rivarol, Voltaire, La Bruyère, Alain... I take advantage of it. It's not completely satisfactory. But who could justify his interest in this or that? His interest in football, overweight ladies, organic chemistry, the novels of Joyce, international politics, crosswords, making money, dainty landscapes — anything. Justification!

JUSTICE

I'm writing this during the second half of January 1963. I notice that the French press is at present devoting space to and showing its solidarity with certain seriously excited protests. To be more specific, I'd better alter that: a section of the French press. For in this area as in everything else, or in this area more than most, some are silent while others shout out and each goes his own way. I can observe, though, that it has been the more open minded, ideologically least backward papers that have been the most genuine in their reports. Two individuals, called Oberg and Knochen, of sinister fame on the other side of the Pyrenees, who were serving an open-ended sentence of imprisonment for their war crimes, have just been released; the Gaullist authorities have decided to free them and send them home — to Germany, needless to say. Oberg and Knochen had played an important role as heads of the Gestapo in France during the Nazi occupation. The legal dossier on their activities contains a terrifying balance, it appears, of 100,000 or so executions — murders, let's say — thousands more deportations and an unverifiable number of torturings and ill-treatment. After the Allied victory, these two thugs of Hitler's were condemned to death; later on they were reprieved and the sentence of death was commuted to one of life imprisonment. Now, for heaven knows what obscure, shady reasons — maybe as a sentimental off-shoot of the recent *entente* between de Gaulle and Adenauer — the French authorities have extended the bounds of their generous forgiveness. Oberg and Knochen are at liberty. And a part of French public opinion, not surprisingly, is up in arms against the official decision.

We must acknowledge that saying not surprisingly is

72

unpleasant. You don't need to be over-apprehensive from a moral point of view to see how harsh it is... Clemency is a virtue which brings credit to its practitioner, we all agree. The two Germans in question — who were undoubtedly responsible for inflicting immeasurable grief on French families throughout those dark years — were termed war criminals and, in theory, received the appropriate punishment. Some would-be purists in jurisprudence could have come up, or still might, with captious contentions as regards the concept of a crime with retrospective force, invented by the victorious side. The academic argument must yield before the terrible reality of the consummate tragedy. Justice came to take on the semblance of revenge; it was justice nonetheless. And now, with the passing of time, the vagaries of diplomacy counsel indulgence. In the abstract no one would have any objection. Mercy and forgiveness finally turn into a praiseworthy gesture. But memory is cruel, particularly if it's the memory of a victim: this is the unsurprising part. And the news that Herr Oberg and Herr Knochen have been returned to their homeland and civilian normality was of necessity to be taken as an insult by the survivors of the Gestapo's iron rule: widows and orphans of those who died at the behest of the oppressor, those who bear on their backs or in their hearts the scars of a painful journey through Hell, men who suffered the insult of an all-powerful humiliation. For all these, the amnesty granted Oberg and Knochen is an aberration. Their bitterness lives on. Ethical considerations are important. But those of us who feel marginal to this problem must agree that, in spite of everything, such cruel indignation may not be just but it is justified. Be that as it may, this is not what struck me most about this incident. The indignant manifestos or communiqués of this or that organisation of ex-combatants, of this or that group of heroes of the Resistance, of the associations of Jewish ex-prisoners are predictable. They are practically a physiological outburst, an automatic reaction, a rejection rooted in personal motives, albeit expressed on a collective basis. There has, in contrast, been a very different kind of protest, a horrifyingly reasonable one, stemming from another source altogether. It was published in *Le Monde* on the 18th of the month. It's signed by two Jesuit priests who are, or at least they were then, prison chaplains at Fresnes. I have no idea whether Father André Legouy and Father Joseph Jaouen, outside or prior to their religious calling were, during the last World War, partisans fighting the intruder, inmates of one of Hitler's concentration camps or close relatives of anyone who tragically suffered such misfortunes. The Jesuits of Fresnes don't make this clear in the course of their arguments. The text they have submitted to the aforementioned Paris newspaper contains in theory nothing more than the simple reflections of a prison chaplain. Not even chaplain actually: just someone familiar with prison life. The style and points raised by Fathers Legouy and Jaouen are lay, profane. We can detect at most one religious premise: enjoined to charity by vow and vocation, the Jesuits confess they cannot be contrary to any kind of clemency, even if the beneficiaries be people such as Oberg and Knochen. But anyone with a normal level of ethical concern would subscribe to this acquiescence to magnanimity, to forgiveness. The particular interest of the text by the *aumôniers* of Fresnes lies elsewhere.

No. No one will argue with the high-mindedness of reducing a sentence: the more shocking the criminal category of the recipient, the more high-minded. Being generous to those guilty of 100,000 murders signifies great generosity. Well then, why couldn't we be just as generous with those guilty of a single murder, fraud, robbery or humble theft? This is where Fathers Legouy and Jaouen give full rein to their feelings. Their pastoral rôle in prison, their direct knowledge of penal conditions in our society, forces them to make bitter comparisons. The denunciation by the Jesuits is neither vague nor abstract but specific. President Coty, who on April 10th, 1958, lifted the death penalty from Oberg and Knochen was the same person who, on October 1st, 1957, consented to the execution of Jacques Fesch, a maladjusted youth accused of having fatally wounded a policeman during a desperate escape. The government which on December 31st, 1959, reduced to twenty years of hard labour the life imprisonment of the two Nazi criminals was the same one which sent a substantial number of F.L.N. rebels to the guillotine and which ordered the legionaries Piegts, Dovecar and Deguelde to be shot. *"Quelle béante disproportion!"*, exclaimed the *aumôniers.* "Not a single one among the criminals at present housed in our gaols, whoever he may be, bears a thousandth of the weight of the crime committed by Oberg and Knocher." And this statement, most likely irrefutable, calls forth some fervent questions, "How can we then allow, without feeling outrage, one of those criminals to be executed? How can we allow, without feeling disgust, a single one of them to be kept behind bars for more than sixteen years?"

Fathers Legouy and Jaouen's criticisms lie not so much in the liberty granted the two Nazis as in the harsh treatment meted out to the rest, particularly the common criminals. The inequality in their treatment is offensive to them: *"Que penser de notre justice?"* I'm not suggesting that the clear-cut arguments brought forward by the chaplains of Fresnes have suddenly brought into question the very foundations of criminal law as we know and obey it. If we look carefully we see they're only attacking a kind of inconsistency which, in their opinion, is shown in the conduct of the state; an inconsistency which has become an injustice through impinging on the lives and liberty of certain people. The authorities are magnanimous towards some and unforgiving towards others and this offends even the most rudimentary ideas of equity. The Jesuits from Fresnes do no more than plead for clemency for the others: for the numerous colourless evildoers, for the routinely corrupt, the mediocrely violent, who have received routine sentences handed down scrupulously by the courts. As a result of humanitarian clichés, well-worn and empty, the image of the common criminal is somewhat remote for us. We can barely picture the automatic severity of the law — if those of us who escape its clutches ever do picture it. And the mournful gloom of the prisons is, for the ordinary citizen, a mere admonitory reference. The truth of all this lies beyond our fortunate everyday life as honourable persons. Only the threat of offences of opinion forces us to think of it occasionally, but not very much. In many countries today political dissent, simple ideological dissent against the constituted powers, brings with it the danger of dreadful sanctions. But let us not pursue this. A prison chaplain — insofar as he does not turn himself into a bureaucrat — is in an excellent position to assess the cruel iniquity of the prison system in civilised societies.

Nevertheless, this problem has other implications. The case of Oberg and Knochen leads us on, almost spontaneously, to that of their colleague Eichmann. The capture, trial and sentencing of this famous slayer of Jews has provided material for spoken or written debate among thousands of people. Eichmann's rôle in the death of millions of Jews was beyond doubt. In spite of everything, the controversy has been sensational: the controversy surrounding the legality of his sentence. Such an argument was symptomatic. Eichmann became a front-page celebrity around the world. We must realise, though, that the scandal stemmed not from the volume of his crimes, but from the nature of those actions described as crimes. It has been a real lesson. In our society it can appear debatable whether the murder of millions of people merits the punishment of the courts; the fate of any convicted and confessed Eichmann is a discussion topic for opposing sectors of public opinion. But no one is against a commonplace petty thief, a sordid villain or someone convicted of murder on personal grounds receiving strict punishment. The unanimity regarding such people — riff-raff — is overwhelming: they must be dealt with. The Eichmanns, Obergs and Knochens of this world do not arouse total agreement: there's always someone to forgive them, and a general indifference which puts up with such forgiveness. Large-scale massacring of Jews, torturing patriots in a neighbouring land, interning dissidents in concentration camps — such are actions which can be squared with illustrious principles and doctrines; theft isn't. Neither theft nor any other form of behaviour on that same level. And when it comes to compassion, the tendencies are the same. Oberg and Knochen have obtained a reprieve thanks to facilities and assistance which would never be offered to a bank clerk imprisoned for unsuccessful embezzlement, or the impatient youth who stabbed his fiancée, or a villainous gangster. They may all be criminals in fact, but not in the same way.

The crimes of war criminals are actually identical in essence to the crimes of peace criminals: murder, pillage, kidnap, wounding, violence against property and persons. The differences, however, are numerous. Most of them highlight the perverse, terrifying side of war criminals. The war criminal acts from a position of power: this comes from having a state force at his disposal as an offensive weapon. He is a military or political leader who acts with impunity in his professional capacity. And, moreover, he acts outside his own state or against dispossessed ethnic minorities. The sense of fighting for a worthy cause against a deadly foe also provides him with a moral intrepidity capable of inspiring the most depraved acts of brutality. The war criminal can rarely resist such inspiration. Since at the same time the chance he is offered is of an exceptional circumstance — war — these repulsive deeds of his will probably multiply and intensify in the climate of hatred, laxity and panic generated at that time. The number of victims, the amount of damage and the corruption of many specific cases reach phenomenal extremes. A common criminal, however athletically destructive, could never match these results. The outstanding figures of the criminal press reports — such as Landru, Al Capone, Doctor Petiot, even those rogues portrayed in sensationalist pamphlets — are nothing more than humble amateurs when compared with an everyday war criminal; none of them even has the peace of mind we can imagine the other possessing.

In relation to war crimes, we can say of them what someone observed regarding high treason or conspiracy to overthrow a regime: they are punishable offences if they fail, and honoured if they succeed. The plotter who fails goes to the gallows or gaol; the successful one to the government, or nearly so. There is no doubt that, had the last world war had a different outcome, those on trial at Nuremburg, the Eichmanns, Obergs and Knochens, would now be parading round Europe bowed down under the weight of their medals and the praise heaped upon them. The awfulness of their misdeeds would have been obliterated by victory. When the thief, the parricide, the rapist, the pathetic figures cut by the transgressors of the criminal code succeed, they can only aspire to elude the snares of the police or the severity of the judges. The truth is that the legal processes looming over both categories are not the same. The war criminals are only subject to the uncertain danger of enemy victory; for the common criminal the state — any kind of state, here or elsewhere — is always a deadly prospect. The state and its laws are a never-failing limitation and threat, and the citizen is always restrained by them: this is the nub of civilian legislation. A citizen becomes a criminal when he clashes with the legality of the state he belongs to. The war criminal is not a criminal because he has infringed any constituted legislation, but for reasons prior to, and overriding, any legislation — reasons which only acquire coercive powers if the criminal fails. The values and interests the crime damages in both cases, in a war or peace crime, are very different. A prosecutor brandishing the criminal code, whatever edition he may have, whether it be enacted here or elsewhere, could not rightfully demand conviction of such as Eichmann, Oberg and Knochen. The criminal codes are drawn up against another order of person. In our misled naivety we believe that the purpose of the criminal code is to maintain justice — or, with a capital letter, Justice — by means of a cleverly progressive system of repression. We believe, since we are led to do so, that the crimes listed in this legal corpus are the entire repertoire of those acts which go against natural law: that notion we term natural law. But the codes do not include the probable brutalities of the Eichmanns, the Obergs, *et cetera*. Those responsible for the gas chambers at Majdanek, the camps at Auschwitz and Buchenwald, do not enter into the calculations of the average legislator. It is not valid to say that they could not enter into the calculations of a legislator of the past; if tomorrow a new criminal code had to be drawn up in a country fond of statute-making, it wouldn't include among its articles the obscene deeds perpetrated by the war criminals either. When a legislator thinks up a criminal code, when the citizen acknowledges therein the prestige of a political safeguard, both legislator and citizen are seeking to root another set of preoccupations in it. It must be ensured that the criminal code is effective and in keeping with the other codes: the civil code, the mortgage law, the commercial code. I am transcribing the names in line with the terminology used in our own country; I trust I make myself clear.

This is all understandable, quite understandable. Luckily the Eichmanns, the Obergs and Knochens are not frequent occurrences: statistically they must be described as anomalies or abnormalities, thrown up by the grotesque, macabre side of life and history. Life and history, however, have a wider surface of normality: an area — the usual one — where there are no gas chambers or concentration camps, but contracts of sale, property registers, money-making. Things such as these are the exclusive object of the legislative structure of the state; for they are, moreover, the economic and social background against which we live. The criminal code is our guarantee of it. The man in the street does not believe it would be possible for his society to survive if these institutions were to collapse, so convinced is he of their importance. Judges, the police and the prisons are a necessary correlative of his belief. With the criminal code on hand to defend him, or trained on him to keep him in line, the citizen feels safe: he feels the system, of which he is part and against which he cannot or will not go, is safe. The law takes on a certain sacred character. This is why, however petty the crime — stealing chickens, a pub brawl — the unfortunate event must be an example: the wrong-doer is punished so that his sentence will act as a warning to others and discourage them from indulging in similar wickedness. But the crime, any crime, also possesses an element of blasphemy, and this is unforgivable.

War criminals break no law because they act outside society. They kill or steal, but standing beyond the every-day values and interests of the society which is their victim. They are, then, the complete opposite of the run-of-the-mill thief or murderer. We must not be surprised, then, if the same society that endured them looks on the war criminals a little as they would an earthquake or tornado, an epidemic, a plague of locusts: as a natural disaster, bloody yet superhuman. They do arouse anger; an anger not dissimilar to that aroused by the Lisbon earthquake in the heart of the rationalist philosopher. In any case, they are eventually filed as an unstoppable calamity. Society is powerless before the arbitrary savagery of the invader, the tyrant, the thug. It is not powerless, however, before the pickpocket, the swindler or perjurer. And time passes, and the despicable side of the war criminal starts to fade. It isn't easy to forget it, but it's no longer a threat. Today, the Eichmanns, Obergs and Knochens, set free, seem harmless: for the time being we cannot imagine them relapsing. We'll never think that of the thief or murderer: they will be dangerous for ever more. The thief and murderer have challenged the laws once, they've lost their respect for them and we fear they will backslide. Society will stand firm against showing them any clemency. Oberg and Knochen will get a better deal. We've just witnessed it. It's shocking, but that's the way it is. A *béante* inconsistency, as the Jesuits Legouy and Jaouen said.

LOVE

"Love? A twelfth-century invention." The phrase —
pronounced, if I am not mistaken, by a respectable scholar
— might seem like a piece of nonsense, but not at all. Indeed
it must be allowed in all its rigorous precision, which brings
us face to face with the social and cultural phenomenon of
troubador poetry. Clearly, there has always been love, some
form or other of love; binding human couples together, ever
since, or almost ever since, humanity has warranted such a
name. Without moving outside the western tradition,
Plato's *Symposium* and Ovid's *Ars amandi* more than bear
witness to this in all their literary magnificence. But not all
loves have been identical, and we should distinguish scrupulously between the different kinds and qualities of love
which have been experienced by people throughout history.
There is no doubt, at least, that whatever it is that we still
call love today — that which was inspired by Beatrice and
Laura, Juliet and Desdemona, Margarida Gautier and Mimi
— was unknown to pagan antiquity as it was also unknown
to the barbarous High Middle Ages and the inscrutable East.
This love is a creation of the Troubadors of Provence,
rounded off and polished up by the Italian poets of the *dolce
stil nuovo*.

Moreover, love spread and took root thanks to literature. I can't remember who it was that said — though you
can bet it was a Frenchman — that a lot of people would
not have fallen in love if they hadn't heard about it earlier.
This is quite often the case, in fact, much more often than
we think. The man and woman of the West, the Euro-
peans, have been making love for centuries, and have
fallen in love according to the dictates of poets without
realising it (and never having read them of course). This is

no exaggeration inspired by a vested interest in literature. We are speaking of love, not of pure and simple fornication, or the institution of marriage, or even the nexus of affection that these relationships can, and normally do, produce. Sexual bonds, family life, mutual affection, are not love. Love, as far as specific feeling is concerned, as we see it in the *Vita Nuova* or *La Dame aux Camélias*, as it is experienced nowadays by the protagonists of romantic fiction and films, as it was expressed by Petrarch and dramatised by Shakespeare, is a completely different thing. In effect, love is only rarely given an absolute dimension; great lovers are the exception. It could almost be said that great lovers have only existed in the world of literature: Werthers, Romeos, Kareninas, Manons are all beings of paper. And when we find one of flesh and blood, they give the impression of being victims of a literary virus.

But, if great lovers are few and far between, we must recognise that the lover — the man and woman who participate moderately in love — is a common type. A common type today, though certainly not 100 years ago, and even less 200 years ago. Love has spread from a few social classes to the others, in a slow and gradual transfusion. Let's not forget that love, in its original state, was courtly love: a thing of aristocrats and their parasites. Provençal poetry and the concept — and feeling — of love it elaborates were, in principle, the patrimony of ladies, knights and the poets in their employ. Later, love was to straddle this first class boundary but remained a vassal of the cultured minorities: writers and readers who, for many years to come, were recruited from the ranks of the well-off. Obviously, reverberations from this were felt by the people. But the disqualified masses were not up to such sentimental delights — or torments. They fornicated or married and that was that. "Rather have I followed common folk's delight," wrote Ausiàs March in the fifteenth century to demonstrate his move away from the practice of select or refined love. People vegetated in common delight, or conformed to conjugal vulgarity, ruled by self-interest or necessity. Great lovers and lovers were nurtured in the higher social spheres. Slowly but surely, first in the theatre and then in the generalisation of literature, love was taught to the masses. Shakespeare's audience could learn to love from the example of Romeo and Juliet, or Othello and Desdemona. Readers of novels, more and more numerous from the eighteenth century onwards, would have still more opportunity.

It was in the age of Romanticism that love achieved its fabulous collective promotion. It is no coincidence that today, in the words of the ingenuous, love is called romantic love. The adjective is doubly justified. On the one hand because romantic writers specialised in the theme of love to the extent of trivialising it in stereotyped formulae; on the other, because in the nineteenth century books penetrated social groups which had been previously impermeable to reading and broadsheets and effusive verses infected the bourgeoisie and an appreciable part of the proleteriat. Films, gossip columns, soap operas and cheap publications finished off the job in our own era. Today, even the most unrefined couple imitate, in their courtship, those sweet scenes absorbed from the cinema screen. They kiss, spoon and pet, following the canons laid down by the movies. Films and love stories make up the sentimental education of the majority of the youth of today, and all this has its roots in the twelfth century, in the intricate, conceptual poetry of the troubadors.

The erotic innovation of the troubadors has, more than anything, caused a readjustment of the place of woman in society. Up until then, a woman's social condition was characterised by the most definite marginalisation. The ancient world, the East, the High Middle Ages, were exclusively male-orientated civilisations. In them, woman was mother or whore, servant or vestal, wife or nun, object to be coveted or scorned, vessel of iniquity or delight of men. Whatever the case, she was outside the frame in which man — the male — placed himself. It was around the twelfth century that a new possibility first appeared for women. It would take too long to give profound details of the causes of the new situation. The fact is that it happened and its literary correlative is the poetry of the troubadors.

Engels saw this most clearly. Courtly love has a distinctive profile, unprecedented in the history of the relationship between men and women. On the one hand, it is a reciprocal love, which means that man needs the participation of woman who, as a consequence, will enter into the erotic world on almost an equal plane to man. Moreover, this feeling ought to be so intense and lasting that both lovers — the woman, therefore, as well — consider separation or non-possession as a tragedy or perhaps the greatest of all tragedies. Clearly, this love was, perforce, a threat to the institution of marriage, a conventional institution subject — especially in the ruling classes — to the requirements of a most apparent family economic strategy. Every marriage was an arranged marriage, and this tendency passed on from feudal society to bourgeois society; and for this reason courtly love and romantic love always came up against social obstacles. The importance of adultery in European literature, and in life itself, has this as its cause from that time on. Love, authentic love, is put to the test in the challenge to convention and vested interests: it either overcomes them or fails tragically in the attempt.

Be that as it may, woman had doubtlessly gained, for good or ill, the new possibility we alluded to: the chance to be a lover, to play an active role — whether fortunate or not is another question — in her relations with man. Literature — a fairly reliable barometer of society — provides us with some significant examples. Literary heroines of antiquity are not heroines through any sense of love: Phaedra, Antigone and Medea are figures who achieve greatness through some or other moral energy, and not for any sentimental decision. On the other hand, Laura and Beatrice, Desdemona and Juliet, Mimi and la Gautier, Emma Bovary, Anna Karenina and countless others are heroines through love. The man-antagonist has, in both spheres, a symmetrical development: Oedipus, Ulysses, Orestes have nothing to do with love, whereas Des Grieux, Werther, Tenorio, Sorel, Adolf, Paul, Othello, Romeo *et al.*, are basically men in love. This is true right up to the twentieth century. In spite of everything, society — western society — has continued to be a male-orientated society. The feudal lady in the first instance, the bourgeois wife later, and eventually any woman, acquired the right to love against hell and high water. Nonetheless, women in a male-orientated society, are never anything more than second-class citizens. Man as lover needs them as lovers; only in the context of this necessity are they equal to men. In the rest of her activities, woman remains relegated to her centuries-old subjugation. Woman's condition in law, as much as the pragmatic evaluation of her, is one of submission. Man has always ruled — in love as in everything — despite appearances.

The twentieth century heralded female emancipation. Emancipation is the word usually used in this context: it's not completely certain, however, whether it is the correct term. Simone de Beauvoir denounced the confusion surrounding the female problem even in the present day and does not accept that emancipation has truly been an emancipation. Militant feminism, since the time of Miss Pankhurst, has advanced a great deal and the incorporation of women on to the shop-floor has gone a long way to eradicate the old male prejudices. Nonetheless, the pressure on women in today's world far exceeds what Emily Pankhurst and her followers could have envisaged sixty years ago. What is important is not that women have the vote — which was, for suffragettes, the social plenitude of their sex — the important thing is that now women have got rid of many subjecting pressures, legal or otherwise, and have come face to face with man in a position of real equality. Equality between men and women is these days relatively tangible and, at this point, love begins to become impossible because courtly or romantic love presupposed the marginalisation of woman. The *inamorata* may or may not love. Her love, her amatory decision, is decisive; but it is only and always in the context that it is sought by the love of a man. The male lover adores and reveres woman. In love a woman as an idol — adored, revered — is no longer a woman. She is not even a woman, but a mystification of woman. This is the cause of the crisis. We can see it in the free and unencumbered behaviour of a sector of urban youth, which eludes the intoxicating influence of the cinema and sentimentalist sub-literature. It is also to be seen in literature.

Literature once again becomes our illustrative reference. Writers, particularly the most wide ranging, are generally very sensitive to social variations of even the most tenuous kind. In the literary output of the twentieth century thus far we can back up those judgments. We observe, for example, a slight unwillingness on the part of poets as far as the theme of love is concerned, which contrasts with their deliberate preference for metaphysical or socially committed themes. You only have to read Valéry, Rilke, Eliot, Claudel or Prévert, Aragon, Nicolás Guillén, Brecht and so many others, to realise this is true. And when love appears in the writing of poets — Eluard, occasionally in Neruda — it is the subspecies of mere sensuous exaltation. The same thing applies to the novel. If the novelist can be bothered about love — for example, Proust, Joyce, Lawrence, Miller — it is in order to reduce it definitively to the opaque mechanism of the flesh. Symptomatic of this is the small space that sentimental tales — in the most noble and accredited sense of the word — about man and woman retain in the books of Malraux, Hemingway, Camus and Silone. When considered carefully, love has no more defence than those instruments of mass culture we have previously pointed out: romantic novels, films, soap operas. This combines with the *chansonniers*, French or otherwise, Jacques Brel or Domenico Modugno, Paul Anka or Nat King Cole, Aznavour or Josep Guardiola, who fill the airwaves with lingering small-change residue of

romantic love poetry. Novels, films, soap operas, singers...
but they have their audience, and a large one at that.

Nevertheless, the end is nigh. Well they all know it; the
maximum diffusion of an idea or fashion coincides with
the moment of its extinction. Love is in such a state: the
last and lowest stage. Our age is putting love out to grass.
The time has come to invent some other love: tomorrow's
love, which will probably not tolerate Don Juan or Juliet,
Bovary or Othello, Werther or Beatrice.

MAN
Man's life, so someone has said, is nothing but a useless passion. We must admit it sounds good; it has a certain romantic elegance to it and we can repeat it among our friends if we want to be thought of as nobly disillusioned souls. But I can't really believe it. In any case I tend to imagine that life ceases being a useless passion when we cease believing it to be so.

MEDITERRANEAN
We inhabitants of the Mediterranean are, in general, very proud of being just that: Mediterraneans. Landlubbers all, we are inspired by a vaguely maritime patriotism which, though certainly far from being harmonious, is as ostentatious and arrogant as any other. I reckon that, when all is said and done, we are entitled to it; an entitlement deriving nowadays more from inheritance than from anything else. When you think about it, the reasons behind this sentiment are not based on any particular satisfaction, justifiable or not, induced by contemplation of the landscape and its intrinsic virtues. We often say that the geography of the Mediterranean is human in scale. This is a lovely expression and one which, moreover, corresponds to our own self-image. Our seaboard landscapes, indeed, have nothing colossal or sublime about them; they are just places where we feel at ease, comfortable, at one with the surroundings. Nothing here is conducive to dreaming, to mysticism or to panic, as you might find in desolate steppes, in grandiloquent mountains, in wild deserts, in luxuriant swamplands. Here everything is accessible, clear, suited to the humble sensuality of every

day, friendly. It is a fact that the same thing could be said of many other places — on land and sea in the world. But any comparison would become meaningless once we passed from geography to the reminiscences and the stock associations suggested by the land and the sea of the Mediterranean. For, ultimately, this is the really important thing; the fact that these shores have been the scenario for the most outstanding episodes of human history. And this, it must be said in all modesty, is not just an opinion. It is what accounts for the fervour of our all-embracing localism.

If we wish, we can proceed directly to demonstrate the point. All we have to do is to go along to the seashore. Any vantage point will do: a cheap beach restaurant or a lavish private villa, a hotel veranda or a rock to perch on. However limited might be our general cultural education, the backward and forward movement of the waves — "la mer, la mer toujours recommencée" — will awake in our memory a vast repertoire of significant connotations, of vibrant and lustrous names, of hauntingly conspicuous events. We could begin, for instance, with the birth of Venus herself, in her lovely, buxom womanhood, amid the miraculous and amazingly fertile foam of the waves. Or with that good fellow Ulysses, canny as they come, the epic hero through and through, stubbornly fighting against his nostalgia for the fire-smoke of home. Then the way would be open for the most gold-tinted variations: from Salamina to Paul Valéry, from Socrates to Sophia Loren, from Napoleon to the *Four Seasons* (Vivaldi's, of course), from Botticelli to Carles Riba, from Cèsar Borja to the Parthenon, from Virgil to Palestrina, from Joan Miró to Thermopylae, from Euclid or St Paul to the miraculous *Dama d'Elx*, and so on *ad infinitum*. The possibilities are endless. Naturally, some sleight of hand is involved: when surveying the imaginary map of the Mediterranean, one has to overlook the African coast or to allow just sporadic concessions regarding that stretch of shoreline — in the cases of St Augustine, for example, or Camus. We shall do well to stake our claim to several outstanding Jews, but Moors, Egyptians and Phoenicians will not fit into our scheme of things. The result of this evocative operation would be most flattering.

The true fact is that the very fundamentals of western civilisation originated by the Mediterranean shore: science, philosophy, art. It is undeniable that these inventions had, to a large degree, roots and precedents of more distant provenance. But it is equally undeniable that everything our ancestors imbibed from the ancient cultures of the Orient was so completely transformed that we can legitimately display it as original. Furthermore, it was our forebears who made these things viable, giving them a definitively universal scope and access. Today's world does not live on the attainments, however admirable, of India, China or the Egypt of the Pharaohs, but rather on the contributions of Greece and Israel: in a word, the Mediterranean. Greece and Israel, together with the products of their more or less harmonious conjunction, constitute the vital, living fabric of the Mediterranean, this hyperbolic Mediterranean, with all its ghosts and its palpable presence, which I am talking about. For many centuries now the Mediterranean basin has no longer had the monopoly on primary creativity and in certain specialities it is now persistently sterile. But we can still unequivocally affirm that the rest of the world is, at bottom, nothing but a Mediterranean colony, or a colony of Mediterranean colonies. Some Tibets still subsist, obstinate in their isolationism. They will soon disappear, though: various parties — ourselves excluded, emphatically — are bringing this about, and *Coca-Cola* and *Das Kapital* are gradually bringing down any last stretches of the great wall built to keep the world at bay. These exceptions aside — exceptions which will anyway be obliterated — the entire moral and physical surface of the earth is impregnated with Mediterraneanism. In the stolid blood of Mr Babbit, without his being aware of it, there runs something that comes from Plato, from St Paul, from Petrarch. The same thing could equally be said of the homologous Russian, Australian or Patagonian Mr Babbits. The Black peoples who are now achieving independence will soon, be they English-speakers or French-speakers, find themselves assimilated.

Nevertheless, we tend not to be looked upon too kindly by people from outside the Mediterranean geography. Sometimes they bestow upon us a rather studied indifference. Perhaps because it's their only way of overcoming their vassal complex. Most foreigners' judgment of us is that we are horrible. With such an attitude they themselves confirm our sense of difference, defining us as an as-it-were ethnically separate group. According to them, we are a jealous, pagan lot, inclined to mirthful obscenity, rationalistic, miserly, garrulous, easygoing, licentious and litigious, split up into tiny and irreconcilable tribes. All of this is true. The only thing is that we don't quite appreciate why such characterisations are necessarily to be taken as criticisms. The non-Mediterraneans still hold some very strange ideas about morality and about life and so they reproach us for things which they ought to admire in us. In any event, we are as we are and that's all there is to it. There have been periods and locations in which the distinctive features just mentioned, and other family traits, enjoyed splendid incarnations: Ancient Greece, obviously, in its heyday; Renaissance Italy. Without such circumstantial luck, those characteristics are reduced to the normal scale of the man in the street, in any little village or great city of these shores. The foreign visitors just can't come to terms with it. In their view, we give off a smell of frying oil and — shame of shames — fried garlic; we are unbearable show-offs, our appearance is utterly plebeian — when it is not excessively aristocratic — and we can barely disguise the bandit that lurks deep inside us all. We, of course, don't give a damn. A foreigner — a *barbarian* — is never right; he might be richer, have more universities, more machines, more food; but, being a barbarian, either more or less enlightened, he can never be right *against* us. That's all there is to it.

It is quite symptomatic that these selfsame foreigners, these insubordinate colonial subjects, should be in the habit of taking every opportunity of journeying to our shores and bathing in their illustrious, liberal waters. Unconsciously, this tourism retains something of the pilgrimage: a kind of pilgrimage back to sacred origins. The smartest ones among them — Goethe, Byron, Stendhal, Shelley, Pound, *et al.* — made the pilgrimage with their eyes wide open. What tempts them is, naturally, this museum, that monument in ruins, the prestige of the glory-burnished toponymy. A trip through the Mediterranean, even if it's only on a fortnight's annual holiday, going from one camp-site to the next, or on pre-programmed itineraries with poverty-stricken guides, is for average tourists a way of getting back to a *Patria* which they have renounced but which at the same time they cannot do without. Roughly speaking, it is like the journey to the Paris of the Sorbonne, of Pigalle and of Saint-Germain-des-Près made by a literate (literate in French) former colonial native of Senegal or of the ex-French Congo. But there is even more to it than that. Although they might not admit it, foreigners come here because they are attracted also by the teeming, sweaty, clamorous spectacle of our cities. Marseilles, Naples, Barcelona, Athens, downtown quarters, festivals, seething crowds — all are perhaps places which repel them, but which seduce them just the same, bewitch them even. An uproarious and gaudy spectacle unfolds before the barbarians' innocent senses. After a few days of living there and drinking in the atmosphere, the foreigner would not be at all surprised, on turning a street corner, to come across Socrates addressing his young pupils, or across a thick knot of citizens heatedly debating — as in the Florence of bygone days — the superiority of Michaelangelo over Leonardo... Anyway, that is what we Mediterraneans believe. Because we, indeed, would not be in the least bit surprised.

MENDACITY

To be a good liar is a very difficult art, which few people manage to practice with any authority or dignity. There are plenty of liars, but in general they are not very good at it; you can always tell they are lying. An untruth ought not to be honourably classed as a lie except when it is perfect, when it offers a reasonable appearance of truthfulness. That is why it is always preferable to tell the truth, the pure unadulterated truth, if ever we are incapable of making up invulnerable lies. Unconvincing lies, moreover, have the disadvantage of discrediting the disseminator. In matters of normal person-to-person relations, the principle of credibility is essential: we must be able to put credence in what we hear, if we are to reach any understanding in conversation. Liars, successful liars, make themselves seem credible; their manipulation of facts or ideas comes across with such a sharp semblance of plausibility that we do not hesitate to take it for the truth. We always know how to deal, or not to deal, with a liar and, even though it might be at our expense, the transaction will always be painless and amicable. The bad liar, on the other hand, puts us in an uncomfortable situation. We know they are lying and credence cannot be sustained — our trust is withdrawn. You can get nowhere with such people; relations will be strained for they rest, if anywhere, on a basis of deception on both sides. A successful lie is as good as the truth. And, I repeat, to tell a good lie requires so many and such demanding qualities of imagination and of ill-intent, that we who are not blessed with such genius ought to desist and to try to be truthful, always and as a matter of principle. Even if telling the truth is unpleasant, as a rule or where we are concerned. On this point, as on many others, expedience corroborates the arguments of the most dyed-in-the-wool moralist.

METAPHYSICS

Despicable Old Spengler — you know, the author *of The Decline of the West* — claimed it was a symptom of the supposed degeneration of our society: the prevalence of the anti-metaphysical spirit constituted, according to him, one of the many signs that attend the passage from a living culture to that kind of terminal arteriosclerosis which is civilisation. Historian and prophet, the German mastermind — because there's no doubt about it, his was a very fine mind — pertinently adduced the parallel cases of other cultures which have suffered the same predicament. Taking an obvious instance, he cited the case of the ancient world, Imperial Rome, which, in contrast with the metaphysical vocation of youthful and flexible Greece, could only tease out moral doctrines, ethical systems, albeit perfect ones, but ones which had no productive roots in the field of philosophical invention. The Stoics and the Epicureans were, for classical antiquity, something similar to what the western world found, or finds, in the French Libertines of the seventeenth century, the enlightened thinkers of the whole of eighteenth-century Europe, the positivists — sociological or socialistic — of the industrial nineteenth century, and the Bertrand Russell-type neo-positivists of not so long ago. The typical intellectual of these arid and definition-bound phases despises transcendental speculation; his critical mentality brings him to opine that the possibilities of the knowledge in whose name he operates cannot extend beyond that which is registered by reason and the senses. Reason and the senses, in combination, make a criterion — the rest is pure fantasy.

Spengler probably believed he was diagnosing an incontrovertible fact because when he was writing his book the West — what we call the West — was inclining, in broad terms, towards a kind of materialism which was more or less coherent and widespread, while metaphysics was collapsing into quite obvious disfavour. These are, I stress, broad terms. Even so, this is not the way that things, or doctrines, have gone. The Spenglerian thesis was easily refutable, in principle, with elementary objections: ever since the days of Romanticism, which was in many respects a reaction against the lucidly rationalist note of seventeenth and eighteenth-century ideology, many European intellectuals had felt within their tender hearts a reawakening of the most stupendous pseudo-mystical preoccupations. A fair proportion of modern literature, precisely that part which set itself up as furiously antibourgeois, from the *poètes maudits* to the Surrealists, is based on a new disregard for reason and on a turbid affection for the Spanish mystics' "dark night of the soul", where uniform gloom prevails. Let us be clear about it: none, or very little, of this had anything to do with religion, or religions. And it is still the case. On close inspection, the metaphysical affinities of contemporary thinkers and poets remain attached to the most recalcitrant atheism, or stray from it with only the slightest vacillations. The assault on reason and on empiricism is never made in the name of the supernatural. Never, or only sporadically, is it the supernatural which supplies the characteristic sign. The supernatural — the religious dimension — is displaced by the irrational. But the fact remains that fantasy — philosophical or pseudo-philosophical fantasy — is recovering lost ground, as Lukács has exhaustively propounded in *Die Zerstörung Vernunft*.

It is curious, for example, that religious concern should loom large in the lucubrations of many contemporary atheist intellectuals. I say religious with all the reservations I can muster. Because, at bottom, if this concern is religious, it is in the topsy-turvy sense. Take André Gide, Jean Paul Sartre, Albert Camus and the minister Malraux — sticking just to French names — and many, many others. A single look suffices to reveal that this whole bundle of atheised religious' preoccupation comes from virtually a single source: Dostoevsky. Kierkegaard is, to some extent, an influence as well, but Dostoevsky above all; and in particular the words and thoughts of some of this novelist's characters. The ideas of Ivan Karamazov or of Kirílov in *The Possessed* have been passed on to the thinkers of recent times as stimuli and imperatives. Ivan Karamazov, Kirílov:

Dostoievskian characters who tend towards metaphysical revolt. It is of no concern whether the revolt is real or not; the important thing is that the impulse should have an initially metaphysical cost. Dostoevsky, the seamless Christian, the bluff adorer of Christ, could not have foreseen what a line his creatures would engender. He could not have imagined that Sartre, Kafka, Camus would emerge from his novels. But so it was. And it is surprising to see how today's atheists are more obsessed with God, with metaphysical realities (or unrealities) than were the deists of earlier times. Voltaire believed in God, and Sartre does not: Sartre, though, is seen to be more preoccupied with God than was Voltaire. Voltaire was anti-clerical, anti-ecclesiastical, rather than anti-religious; Sartre attacks the Church and churches for all he is worth but, in the last analysis, the image of God looms over his thinking.

This mention of Sartre makes it worthwhile to recall an observation made by Erik Peterson about Heidegger's existentialism: his anthropology is shot through with a secularised version of Protestant theology. Peterson goes on to say that a mischievous spirit might wonder whether Sartre's plays were not, in reality, merely a ploy of Christian dogmatists to promulgate, under a thin skin of atheism, some basic notions of Lutheran theology. We can overlook the jocular note in Peterson's remark. The point is undeniable. Maritain himself has stressed that all the great modern metaphysical systems have scarcely or only apparently been able to shake off the influence of theology: the questions which engaged the theologians — old-fashioned theologians — are the same as those which still intrigue philosophers — metaphysicians — today. Because the bottom line is this: metaphysics — Metaphysics — is rearing its head. The anti-metaphysical spirit envisaged by Spengler still enjoys amongst us, as I remarked, a certain operability in neo-positivism, Marxism, private scepticism. But, despite everything, the metaphysical mood prevails. When we open a history of philosophy and look at the chapters on our times, the prominent names are those of metaphysicians. The metaphysical revival is not restricted to the philosophical terrain: all the currently fashionable modes of irrationalism, even the most idiotic of them — newspaper astrology, quackery, lyrical poetry — are to be reckoned as part of the same trend. Perhaps metaphysics is perpetually renewed. The *metaphysical* will be with you always...

It is the facts which refute, confute Spengler. That is the pity of it!

MONEY

I don't understand those who say they despise money. It's so hard to earn!

NATIONALISM

The Aguiló Catalan Dictionary records a word which we might call precursory: "nationist". Don Marià Aguiló documents it with a sentence from a tome called *Lumen Domus*, which is a text unknown to me and of mistily uncertain date. Doubtless, our eminent savants know all about *Lumen Domus* and it is even quite probable that, were I to rummage now in my library, I would find for myself some exact reference in one unlikely monograph or another. I don't know, and it doesn't really matter. The tiny fragment of *Lumen Domus* reproduced by Aguiló goes as follows:

> Whenever the preaching orders of Catalonia dare to complain and speak with appropriate zeal about their fellow countrymen, they are immediately described as outlaws and "nationists".

One thing to get clear: outlaw, here, means biased; we must not read too much into it! From the general flavour of the language and from the distinctly clerical tone of the quotation I believe we can date the reference as pre-nineteenth century. That much is clear; so there is no need for me to get out of my chair to go and consult any explanatory bibliography.

Even if it is no earlier than the eighteenth century, the text — that word nationist — is a significantly early occurrence. The term is equivalent, strikingly close, to *nationalist*. The particularly noteworthy thing, the feature to be stressed, is that the Catalans should be charged as nationists long before nationalism ever appeared on the ideological map of Europe. It is of no significance that the reference in *Lumen Domus* should be restricted to the

closed community of the Dominican Order; it is as Catalans that St Dominic's friars are taunted with the word in
question. Thus it is that in the Catalan language this
derivation from *nation* — with the addition of the obviously meaningful suffix — pre-dates the occurrence of the
word, I am convinced, in any other European language.

I cannot guarantee this assertion; it is pure suspicion.
But I should be very, very surprised to be proved wrong.
Because when one considers the matter carefully, there
were few European peoples in such propitious conditions
as our own to become nationalist — nationalist, I stress —
before nationalism arose as doctrine and determination at
the beginning of the nineteenth century. In this we were
ahead of everyone else. Ever since the Middle Ages we
have been a people *providentially* — if you will permit the
adverb — predestined to an implacable sort of nationalist
vocation. The good friar who was the author of those lines
in *Lumen Domus* adduced by Aguiló revealed this in a confused, instinctive way.

Now we must take the term nationalism — nationism,
as the friar would have said — with a bare-faced disregard
for its historical connotations. We also have to reduce its
scope to what the Dominican of *Lumen Domus* was really
referring to: "to dare to complain and speak with appropriate zeal" regarding the attributes of his own nation.
Complaining, on the one hand; *being zealous*, on the other
— and zealous, obviously, to the point of over-zealousness.
All nationalisms are precisely that: the expression of grievances and claims for the restoration of rights. Behind
every patriotism, pertaining to whichever country, there
stands a watchful suspicion directed against neighbouring
countries. There would be no such thing as patriots if they
did not have rival patriots to confront. But perhaps our
use of the word nationalism implies a rather special form
of patriotism: an aggrieved and consequently more aggressive patriotism. Because of the grievances, it articulates
complaints; and the accompanying *zeal* is precisely an outburst of aggression. As I was saying, our people had more

reason, more natural — and dramatic — propensities to engage in lamentation and claim their rights — both elements in defence of fellow countrymen and themselves —, than any other peoples in their vicinity. A simple reflection or summary examination of what we refer to as peoples in Europe after the fifteenth century would explain why this was so.

Other European peoples, from that time to Napoleon's day, are either fully-fledged, that is fulfilled — or in the process of fulfilment — in their *normal* destiny as a people; or else they are frustrated as a people to an almost lethal degree and, as a consequence, incomplete, unfulfilled. We can illustrate this with a graphic example: the French are *fulfilled* as a people; whilst those in the territories of Occitania are a *frustrated* people. The whole ethnic and cultural make-up of the continent could, more or less, be divided according to this classification, up until the eve of the Romantic period. There were those peoples who were on the ascent, consolidating their personality, asserting their living hegemony among their entourage. Then there were others, the latter and then others who did not attain the collective maturity implicit in their roots, who began to fade, to lose definition and vertebration, merging in with the dominant people. When nationalism takes off, when true nationalism — be it from above or below, centripetal or centrifugal — animates European society, then the two classes of peoples referred to enter into a new phase of political consciousness and ourselves as well. We, however, before this, before the true surge of nineteenth-century nationalism, had been neither fully-fledged nor frustrated as a people. That we were not fully-fledged is perfectly obvious; the last king of the house of Trastámara (Ferdinand the Catholic), deliberately or not, blocked all routes that the Catalan-speaking lands might have followed towards separate plenitude by incorporating them within a foreign political orbit. While we did not enjoy fulfilment neither did we become a frustrated people for we were not destroyed or extinguished as a community. Our historians tend to apply the label of decadence to the period which opens with the Trastámara dynasty of the fifteenth century — at the very least with the Emperor Charles (1516-1556) — and closes with Aribau's verses and the beginnings of the *Renaixença*.[1] In fact, the matter is too complex to be so summarily categorised. It is true that there were, in that period, some fundamental derelictions, notably in the renunciation of fidelity to the Catalan language; in the equivocal submission to the myth of Spanish kingship; in many other defeatist attitudes.

Even so, it cannot be said that our identity as a people was being diluted, certainly not, at least — and I return to my earlier example — in proportions anywhere near comparable with the case of Occitania. We were not achieving notable fulfilment, but at the same time we were not frustrated. In recent years we have witnessed how Catalan historiography has reappraised our eighteenth century, discovering there moral and material energies which the simplistic tag of decadence disguised, and which were at the root of revival and renewal in the nineteenth century. Thus there has been a rectification to the image of a featureless phase of eighteenth-century Bourbonisation, marked by the alternative of defeat or defection; economic revival and the enlightened spirit of some of our key eighteenth-century figures are an enormously powerful counter-balance to this cliché. But we should remember too the rebellions of the *Germanies* and the uprising of 1640, and the War of Succession, which are also spasms of vitality, and not the only ones.[2] In books and documents, in many tiny incidents of everyday life, the Catalans demonstrated, however intermittently, their refusal to be totally extinguished as a people. And it was this instinctive resistance, this potential in reserve, which made them, or enabled them to be, nationalistic. A fully-fledged people had no need to feel nationalistic; nor did a frustrated one. The former has nothing to express grievances or demands about while the latter is too enfeebled to be able to. The patriotism of the strong and healthy peoples was nourished on pride and heroic memories and, if occasionally it was pricked into combative outbursts, then it was against another strong and securely constituted people on equal terms and equal footing; as is clearly seen in the international wars of the sixteenth, seventeenth and eighteenth centuries, struggles between national monarchies incarnating the expansionism of the front-rank peoples.

It is not, then, a question of the kind of nationism which, for the Dominican of the *Lumen Domus*, distinguished the Catalans of that era; rather than grievances and zeal, what we see is arrogance — the arrogance of the victor or of the vanquished, whichever. Some of Quevedo's writings against the French are a good illustration of this. Those other peoples who drowsed in their frustration could not even muster any patriotism, except on the scale of individual municipalities. In contrast with both of these, the Catalans were in a position to become nationistic, with an almost premonitory facility. We can easily imagine what must have provoked the remark in *Lumen Domus*: an argument between monks of different nationalities, in which our compatriots stood out because of the committed fervour with which they defended themselves on questions of national pride. The sense, giving rise to similar commentary, could well be imagined in any other context, in quite different circumstances, whenever Catalans confronted people of different origins. The foreigner who witnessed such outbursts of concerted particularity would doubtless be amazed, struck by what he considered excessive enthusiasm. Whence the outlaw tag: we were looked upon as sectarian, a sectarianism deriving from a sense of nationism. The Catalans of the period of decadence were pained or disturbed by a feeling of being left behind when they still thought they had the strength to ensure an honourable place for themselves among the full-grown peoples. It was a belief which did not correspond totally with reality, but neither was it too far-fetched. Which is why the nationistic reaction was not only understandable but even fatefully ordained.

The Catalans dared to complain and spoke with the appropriate zeal whenever they looked upon their condition as a people, which was neither success nor failure. To an extent, then, nationism amounted to a kind of nationalism *avant la lettre*. What I am unsure about is whether this nationism was, ultimately, the best possible preparation to give subsequent nationalism a smooth and flourishing course. When all is said and done, political Catalanism has probably never attained the highly strung and earnest temper of true nationalism. It gives the impression of having been stuck in the nationist phase: the early promise, mentioned earlier in passing, was not fulfilled. I cannot dwell here on an analysis of the manifold, contradictory repercussions of nationalism among European peoples. What is beyond dispute, though, is that in our midst there arose a set of circumstances which were, hypothetically, conducive to a powerful surge of nationalism. The idea of our normality as a people could have become as forceful an incentive to full collective recovery as the prospects of its success were daunting. But despite what the outraged bluster of dyed-in-the-wool opponents from the Spanish heartlands might have led one to believe, Catalan nationalism never was a virulent, resolute force. There is no doubting our nationalist vocation; adversity pushes me implacably in that direction. Like the friars of the *Lumen Domus*, we complain and speak with the appropriate zeal regarding the grave problems peculiarly affecting us. But this is as far as it goes. And nationalism is, precisely, the step which follows on, taken decisively and with some exasperation. I shall not claim that we have not had our nationalists, especially in the Principality of Catalonia, a few in Valencia, very few in the Balearic Islands, two or three north of the Pyrenees. Numerically they have not amounted to much. Nationism, on the other hand, is a widespread and consistent feeling throughout our territories. I do not pass judgment; facts are facts, and I respect them sincerely. But I do see in it a very clear sign of anachronism. To be nationistic was an understandable, logical stance in the seventeenth or eighteenth century. It was nothing of the sort by the nineteenth century. Nowadays, to be nationalistic is also an anachronism. The only thing is that there are peoples who, deep down, can still be nothing except that. It is absurd. Pathetically absurd.

NOVELS

A good friend of mine, very young and very sharp — endowed, I mean to say, with that ingenuous curiosity or that curious ingenuity which enables one, with utmost honesty, to find earth-shattering excitement in discovering the obvious — has explained to me how dazzling he found his first reading of Dostoevsky. It is certainly true that being astounded by the fabulous Fiodor Mikhailovich is nothing unusual: it counts among the major inevitabilities in the field of literature; and it is not this particular thing that has given me the idea to write the present piece. What has surprised me, on the other hand, is a remark made by my friend, perhaps a tentative objection to the Russian novelist, made with admirably straightforward seriousness. "Don't you find," he said, "that some of Dostoevsky's characters speak and act as though they were older than the age the novelist makes them?" Doubtless, the moral maturity in the psychology of Dostoevskian creatures — or in the way this is portrayed — comes across with such overwhelming emphasis, that if we compare it with the psychology of those around us, even with our own, we find it unconvincing, at least in some cases; and such a comparison, obviously, seems bound to be made.

I find myself unable to side with my friend's veiled reproach. It is some time since I frequented, at least with full attention, the pages of Dostoevsky and I find it impossible, just from memory, to put a definite age to the figures of Raskolnikov, Alexei Karamazov or Prince Myshkin. But even if in fact it is so, and those (or other) Dostoevskian characters seem, or really are, more *adult* than could be considered normal or predictable, the last case I should have chosen to complain about in this matter would be that of the author of *The Damned*. I insist that in these reflections I can only have recourse to a vague and distant general view of Dostoevsky's fictional universe — without concrete details, without checking information, without great concern for precision — the view that remains after quite a lot of secondary components are forgotten. The humanity that peoples the great Slavonic author's books, looked at from a distance and as a single whole, has about it something of uncompromising phantasmagoria. His best characters, rather than men and women, are individualized centres of psychic intensity. The physical dimension — body, ageing, illness — matters less than their passion. Any implausibility, where it exists, becomes hard to define and does not disturb us at all. The struggle between Good and Evil, or between multiple manifestations of Good and Evil, Dostoevsky's recurrent theme, scarcely requires any concretion beyond the mere contrasting of tragic attitudes.

Nevertheless the problem remains, plain and unaffected by such considerations. And not just concerning Dostoevsky. The defect of *overadult* characters occurs frequently in novels of all periods and all places. Adolescents, more so young children, who move in and out of works of imagination tend to be made grown up, too adult, in their speech and actions. The novelist confers upon them thoughts and adventures which the reader, in his or her personal experience — judging from the standpoint of experience — cannot view as normal for those stages of development. One cause of this false focus, the most obvious, has to be the basic fact that the writer is an adult who is consequently inclined to carve out his characters from within himself, as a reaction that unburdens him of something; the character is duly made in the image and likeness of the author. It is thus to be expected that distortions will occur, sometimes — in the cases of mediocre novelists, let us be honest — really awkward distortions. It is worth stressing, too, that if young children appear so rarely and adolescence so infrequently in great novels (Dickens excepted?), it is surely due to an obvious tendency to avoid the attendant dangers, to avoid the danger of getting them wrong. Consider incidentally how certain writers — for instance Proust, in some passages — get round this: through evocation, evocation referred backwards through the adult.

Whenever we would discuss the reality of fictional characters, we shall definitely have to refer to Flaubert's compendious affirmation that "Madame Bovary c'est moi!" Another aspect of plausibility is immediately brought into question, this time concerning gender. If Emma Bovary *was* Flaubert, and Albertine was (perhaps in a different way) Proust, is not the outcome bound to be a deception, or in the final analysis a dubious approximation? And if, despite everything, we find it convincing, must it not be because we, male readers, are not females and are thus unable to corroborate the live authenticity of the fictional invention? We ought, indeed, to be more circumspect and not to reduce novels to an all consuming transposition of autobiography. We should remember, in line with Thibaudet, that the female collections, the reference dictionaries for the women in the creative enterprise of Balzac's novels, were Madame de Berny, Laura d'Abrantés and Madame de Castries. Second-hand material, observed in the world around us, plays a powerful role in the make-up of characters. But autobiographical pressure persists, lurks watchfully, constantly, never to be evaded. And even if, when all is said and done, Madame Bovary were not Flaubert — the relationship can be predicated for all characters in relation to their authors — if Emma were not Flaubert, I maintain, she would still be the idea that Flaubert had of the dreary provincial adulteress. However much he might have copied from a real model, however much he might have relied, like Balzac, on the confidences of *real* women, the intimate fibre of the char-

106

acter would still have been, for sure, a projection of himself.

It would be curious to take a number of first-rate novelists and to establish how the ages of their characters — the age that we are told or that they seem to be — parallel the authors' ages at the time of creating them. I believe we would come, in quite a number of cases, to some interesting observations. In two senses, however. On the one hand, as I have been pointing out, the presence of the writer, of his personal chronology, imposed upon his characters, assimilating them into it more or less reluctantly. On the other hand, though, the characters' ages could often explain a hint of something revealingly linked not to the author's real age, but to his psychological age. I will clarify this now with an example from Stendhal. Stendhal wrote his novels when he was past forty; Fabrice del Dongo and Julien Sorel, though, bear no ill effects from this; they are absolutely credible and their attitudes and reactions correspond to the eighteen or twenty years that Henri (or Arrigo) Beyle has conferred on them. Has Stendhal managed to repress his own feelings and, now in his maturity, reconstruct unrestrictedly how it feels to be very young? I think that a different hypothesis is more probable: Stendhal never grew up beyond twenty; he was stuck — mentally, morally, sentimentally — at that age. He was the everlasting young Napoleon look-alike, dashing or ambitious, romantic and stubborn, which his characters are; or, if you prefer, his characters are diverse but not divergent, imagined (or imaginary) facets of the real Stendhal, of that Stendhal who was a living anachronism.

If we consider it carefully, the problem of age is only one tiny part of the problem of the character's complexity. The superficial reader usually finds it hard to accept the pathetic and confused nature of many fictional characters. Men and women are not like that is how the protest runs. And one wonders: are they, are we really *like that*? Each and every formula, each and every novelistic technique, even the most scrupulously realistic in intent, always

107

entails *exaggeration*: that much is undeniable. What the writer does, in general, is just to relate the significant events concerning his character but then, in isolating and highlighting them, he tends to produce an effect which is larger than life, inflated to some degree, but unavoidably so. But this evident exaggeration does not prevent the *truth* of the character — and of incident — being taken at face value. There is not that much difference between a man in a novel, a figment, and a man in the street, a real person, considered as human types. At bottom, the man in the novel is just the man in the street seen, or analysed, by a novelist. Seen without his being aware of it, as we might say. Potentially, all people are Dostoevskian characters and I mention these in particular on account of their reputation for being bizarre and out of the ordinary: we are all potentially Dostoevskian characters, waiting for a Dostoevsky to come and pick us as subjects. Our tiny experiences of misery and our tiny virtues, of which we scarcely take notice within the daily routine, would come out as tremendously, epically heart-wrenching beneath the gaze, beneath the minutely, violently amplifying optic of a great novelist.

We should also apply this reflection, in small degree, to the matter of the characters' ages. The young children and the *adultified* adolescents we meet in books are not then such adults as we first thought. Without dismissing other factors, mentioned here or not, the issue of complexity has to be taken into account. For, even when we are grown up, we do not *see* ourselves living; we are not aware of the vast dramatic flow of time and of things that constitute our lives. Did we see ourselves, did we have that awareness when we were children or adolescents? And yet our lives then must have been tense, darkly shot through with urges and desires, question marks and contradictions. We do not see ourselves living, immersed as we are in our lives, concerned to live them; we do not normally need to formulate in thoughts, in words or in any kind of lucidity all the many moods or feelings that seethe within our mortal frame; quite often we even have no sensation that we are capable of feelings. The novelist's job is to make up for this distraction, for this deficiency of *awareness*.

ORDER

The disorder *versus* injustice dilemma has used up a lot of ink ever since Goethe first posed it, as we are told, in his decoratively categorical way. The monster of Weimar asserted: "Injustice is preferable to disorder." Doubtless he had impeccable arguments to justify his preference. I do not know whether or not the author of Faust, when he wrote that, was minister to the Duke Charles Augustus, a post which he occupied for several years and with ample devotion; in any event, that statement strikes me as being, literally, ministerial. I suspect that it would be endorsed to the letter by a great many people of the most diverse and contradictory political persuasions who, through one circumstance or another, find themselves perched at the top of the greasy pole of power. Posed as a dilemma, or dichotomy, or whatever you like to call it, the binomial contrast disorder–injustice is nothing but a monumental fallacy. We only have to consider it for a moment to be struck by an initial, unquestionable objection when we enquire, ingenuously, whether injustice of any kind is not immediately, in itself, disorder. And indeed, perhaps injustice is the worst of all forms of disorder because it gnaws away at and corrupts the very foundation of order which, if the cliché is to be believed, is justice itself.

But all that is rather vague and hard to grasp. The word justice is too easily manipulated, a constant equivocation. It will be better if we focus on the problem from the angle of order. And what, when we weigh it up carefully, is order? For the Goethes of this world, no doubt, order means simply holding on to their ministerial posts. The definition is peremptory and rather brutal; I don't believe it is inaccurate, however. Holding on to positions as ministers or as anything else — it doesn't matter what, land-owners or administrators, bailiffs or bureaucrats, canons or salaried staff — this is the situation order has to pre-serve. Law and order, order in the streets: public order. This is why fear about upsetting the established order is a very widespread sentiment. And it is logical. No society can live in chaos — so it has to live in order. Only a certain sort of uncontrolled and febrile anarchistic mentality could stand out, in principle and systematically, against order. The question, nevertheless, is not focused on the necessity or otherwise of order in the abstract as a cohe-sive force in society. What is open to criticism at a certain point in the argument is one or other concrete manifesta-tion of order. One or other particular order, one estab-lished order or another, becomes open to criticism when it collides with justice. I stress what I pointed out earlier: the word justice is basically vague.

But the Goethes of this world know what it means: they can distinguish between justice and injustice, even if only fortuitously. And they allow the possibility that order, their order, might come to stand in contradiction to jus-tice. Their reasoning is simple: between injustice and dis-order one must choose injustice since an unjust order will always be better, infinitely better, than chaos. The argu-ment could be refuted easily but it is not that which con-cerns me now. What I am interested in here is the reaction of the Goethes. For they, in effect, by disregarding injus-tice and clinging to order as they explicitly proclaim, are recognising that the order in question is an aberration. Only private pragmatism leads them to behave, or to think, in these terms.

The seriousness of the matter, then, does not reside in their wanting to maintain and to retain at any cost certain social privileges, but rather in the fact that it is a Goethe who should wish to dress up the idea in an affirmative vague-judgment. The people of order, out of ignorance or innocence, tend to have a clear conscience on this matter. It is more than likely that Duke Charles Augustus of

Weimar never felt the slightest bit uneasy about the legitimacy of the order over which he ruled. The corner shopkeeper, the income tax inspector, the parish priest and so many others, have so far never doubted the natural inevitability of the order into which they fit and only accidentally do they see it as being in any way opposed to justice. But something quite different is to be expected of the Goethes. Perhaps not of the minister Goethe, obviously. Minister Goethe did the right thing — "render unto Caesar what is Caesar's" — to proclaim the advantages of injustice over disorder. He, when all is said and done, had a professional interest in the established order, in the powers that be. The distressing thing is that Goethe was not only minister to a second-class dynast; he was, over and above that, something much more. And this is the reason why his duty was to respond differently. I have detected among the most fashionable political progressivism a tendency to admire Goethe as a member of their catalogue of precursors. Lukács has written a whole book — a very boring book — to demonstrate the point. I have no very strong opinions on the matter. But if preferring injustice to disorder is not apocryphal — and I cannot guarantee the authenticity of the sentence — then the Olympian German poet ought to come in for some reservations on this particular subject. We couldn't absolve him without feeling rather uneasy. He was a clear-sighted man and he knew what he was saying.

PARDON

The matter is fairly straightforward: pardon, as a moral act, is frankly in decline. We could even go so far as to say that in present society, the only practices which retain the name of pardon and come close to the old notion seem to be nothing more than one form or another of penitential remission: amnesty in legal terms and sacramental absolution in religious terms. However, neither amnesty nor sacramental absolution are self-administered; they are exercised by the institutions of state and church through their servants. All things considered, people nowadays do not pardon: the notion of what it means to forgive and be forgiven has been lost. In the area of personal relations between individuals that sort of moving, somewhat theatrical crisis which liberates tensions, reconciles people and constitutes forgiveness is a rare occurrence. We could read an immense number of contemporary novels and dramas without coming across a single one of those scenarios which were so abundant and exaggerated in the literature of times gone by. Nowadays we have restricted pardon to the realm of a routine and inconsequential nuisance: we only ask each other for forgiveness — and we only give it ourselves — when we step on our neighbour's foot, when we rudely and annoyingly push someone in the street, when we say "Pardon me. Do you have the time?"

Genuine pardon, pardon which has a certain ethical grandeur, is always to be found in the case of an important affront. We forgive offences; we forgive our enemies who, by definition, offend us simply by existing. And an offence can only be considered to be exactly that — an offence — when it is felt as such: that is to say, when the act of which it consists has wounded us to the extent that it brings about a reaction of hatred. I do not believe that I am exaggerating when I use the word hatred. There are some people who are terribly offended by things which others would greet with absolute indifference; the capacity to lose one's temper when faced with the same cause varies greatly from person to person. However, when someone feels offended there is no doubt that the psychological mechanism of their attitude can be classified as hatred. The offence arouses a feeling of resentment towards the offender in the offended person, a bitterness which tends to express itself in some sort of violent reply. In other words, the offended party tries to take revenge. One will either succeed or not; that depends upon the circumstances. Nevertheless, the desire and the aim are vengeance.

The opposite to vengeance is pardon. All the merit of pardon stems from this aspect: the offended person, calculating all the insidiousness of the offence, feeling the pain of the hatred which is natural to it, overcomes the rancour of vengeance. Forgiveness is a victory over oneself. It is clear that not all actual acts of pardon have such a justification. There are those who are quick to forgive offenders because they are incapable themselves of hatred, or because they are tired of hatred. I'm not talking nonsense here. Both hatred and love affect people in the same way: hatred and love are *activities*, psychological movements which need to be nourished at every moment in order to subsist. In the same way that it is not easy to love, it is also not easy to hate. For that reason indifference, which is more comfortable, is also more usual. Though we may give it a thin covering of love or hatred, it never ceases to be indifference, apart from some exceptional moments. I am convinced that many acts of forgiveness were nothing more than the end of hatred brought about by impotence or fatigue. True pardon, on the other hand, presupposes the complete mordacity of hatred, a tough exclusive feeling of resentment. The anger of the father of the prodigal son — a sublime example of forgiveness — was in reality incommensurable with the facts; or at least it appears this way to us today because of the prestige and devotion which paternal authority demands. The supreme magnanimity of that biblical figure depends in the end on the ferocity of the previous resentment (an offended father!) which had been overcome.

It is possible that the present decline of pardon is due to the visible loss of validity experienced by Christian values within our society. Although pardon is not exclusive to Christian ethics, it would appear indisputable that Christianity gave it new spiritual dimensions which were foreign to the morals of the philosophers. For centuries, the western world has *lived* pardon through the Christian conception. We cannot deny therefore that, to a certain extent, the propensity for forgiveness has declined as the Christian sentiment of virtue has weakened. All the same, I am not completely certain that this is the most decisive factor in this phenomenon. If people were not to forgive through lack of a vocation for charity, the absence of pardon would be translated into a firm persistence of hatred. There being no charity, hatred would subsist. One would not forgive one's aggressors and the ill will would remain unanulled. The truth is that nothing of that sort happens. People do not forgive but neither do they hate. And if we stop for a moment to think about it, we come to the conclusion that people, including ourselves, do not forgive *because* they do not hate. The decline of forgiveness is, in the end, a decline in hatred.

The problem becomes more complicated. Does this mean that the resentment which is awakened by an offence now takes on more captious or less harsh aspects? I don't know. Perhaps we should look to pride for an explanation? Our age probably creates a human being of a more proud nature than previous times: proud in the sense of disdaining the links of social and cordial solidarity of which the deep substance of human life has always been made. The man of today avoids associating himself with his fellow men as *fellow men* — and I write fellow men

115

fully conscious of the Christian resonance of the words. We tend to establish a void between each one of us and everyone else: an insuperable distance. In any case, a distance which an offence rarely manages to overcome. What is more, even were the offence to succeed in affecting us, why should we accept it as a motive for resentment? Hatred too is a form of association, a connection. We try to make ourselves impervious to the offence since in this way we become impervious to hatred: we become impervious to solidarity. By not hating the person who offends us, that is to say our enemy, we eliminate him with tremendous rapidity. Indifference is our ivory tower. In these conditions, pardon has no reason for existence. The parable of the prodigal son has become an anachronistic image, affectionately archaeological, in ruins. There is nothing that can be done about it.

PEOPLE

Usually, when we say people we never, or hardly ever, mean ourselves. I say people and mean others. That's right: people are others. By definition people are others, not me. We refuse to see ourselves submerged, or subjected, to the vague concept of group, a muddled, confused human hotchpotch. Not even if we're there, not even if we have formed part of that crowd in person, do we acknowledge it. Other words such as nation or gang or society or party or team, when they refer to us too, seem right to do so; they even allow a possessive adjective — my nation, my gang, my society, my party, my team — which accentuates the fact of our belonging to them. However, we don't say my people, unless the term people is being used as an exact synonym for one of these other words. People is something different. The word, standing on its own like that, sets up a differential distance between the person saying it and the conglomerate referred to. People were doing this or that, people were shouting, people leaving the football match, or the pictures, people at the demonstration — this kind of expression is often used by the very folk who were there and who, nevertheless, by speaking thus, dissociate themselves. Each and every one of those present could say the same. And they'd all be right. The concept of people only emerges once we've moved away, albeit in our minds. To be more precise: insofar as we've turned to the concept of people, we have stopped forming part of the people, we are no longer the people, regardless of whether our physical presence is still there among the crowd. By thinking in such terms we have automatically detached ourselves. Maybe because reflection cuts us off. It can be stated, in any case, that people exist only so long as those assembled don't think of it: they don't think that they are individuals assembled together. With nation, gang, society, party, team and so forth, there is a sense of having come together as a community; not with people. Conglomerations of human beings, brought together by chance, shapeless, rooted in inertia or enthusiasm, the throng braying at a football match, roaming round or hiding away in the cinema, elated mobs of hotheads and a quiet funeral procession are, for us, people. And we're there often, nearly always on one occasion or another. It's true that as we can only talk of people once we're no longer part of them, we sometimes have the impression that we're on the outside, essentially on the outside. But that's a delusion. There's no doubt that people mean others — and each one of us.

PLAGIARISM

I came across these words in an old article by Josep Pla (*Revista de Catalunya* 4 [1927], p. 570):[3]

> Plagiarism had never been considered something which was to be criticised. It is nowadays, however, since the writer who plagiarises is considered by his peers to be a man who breaks the rules of commercial chivalry.

Pla, according to his reputation, has always been a staunch defender of plagiarism and — if we are to believe some of his critics and certain confessions by the man himself — even a great practitioner of plagiarism. That is clearly taking things too far; Pla, rather than plagiarising, has hankered after the possibility of plagiarising; rather than defend plagiarism, he has mocked the originalist pretensions which characterise literary and artistic activity in our time. In any case, phrases such as those quoted above expound very particular ideas about the problem. Ideas which, it goes without saying, have discreetly scandalised those honourable persons who have enlisted in the ranks of the pen with priestly illusions. It is perfectly understandable that the writer from the Empordà should react in this way to the question of plagiarism; in his conception of literature, free from transcendental whims, the scruple about copying is nothing less than a hysterical load of cobblers. There are perhaps two reasons which form the basis of the justification which Pla gives for plagiarism. One is historical — "the ancients continually plagiarised each other without respite"; the other is empirical — that we should take advantage of what is useful in the efforts of others, since "between us all we cover everything". On the other hand, behind the scenes, the weary voice of Ecclesiastes unceasingly reminds us that there is nothing new under the sun...

All the same, the text cited at the beginning of this note has an insinuating ring which we should pay attention to. The plagiarist, says Pla, is a writer who "breaks the laws of commercial chivalry." Could this be one of the strongest reasons for the repugnance towards plagiarism which predominates in modern literature? It is obviously not the only one. Factors and circumstances which are intrinsic to contemporary cultural evolution come together here. The progressive accentuation of individualism which Europe has contemplated since the Renaissance has had a profound effect on the professional ethics of the man of letters. Without doubt, literary work has always been or tended to be personal creation, work which is irrevocably expressive of the one who creates it. Nevertheless, this too has not always manifested itself, or tended to manifest itself, either in the same way or with identical intensity. Throughout history the trade of writing has had many diverse and diverging social implications; and it is a notorious anachronism to suppose that the literary attitude of Horace was the same as that of a Victor Hugo, that of a Kafka similar to that of a Goliard or a Troubadour, that of a pious medieval hagiographer comparable to that of a Rimbaud. By contrast with the intellectual habits of the Medieval period the Renaissance, speaking in general terms, of course, introduces a new sense of value of the personality which is accentuated in the case of the lay writer. The poet, the narrator, the philosopher do not limit themselves to writing *a* work — which could often circulate as an anonymous piece, valid in itself — but rather they aspire to produce *their* work: a work which carries the very personal print of its author, unable to be confused with any other work by any other author. The aspiration to originality is accentuated further as time goes by: first subjectivist Romanticism, then the *fin-de-siècle* period and finally the anarchic euphoria of the isms mark successive leaps in that direction. The process of individualism in the field of culture necessarily has to be related to a parallel process which functions in the arrangement of the economic — socio-economic realities of our world. The trajectory followed by the bourgeoisie for the last 600 years illustrates it well enough. Economic individualism, which constitutes the renewing force of this class in its period of ascension, had to express itself in another son of individualism, artistic, literary, philosophical and therefore insane. In the first stage, from Erasmus to Voltaire, from Montaigne or Descartes to Diderot, bourgeois ideology leads a noble, liberating combat in preparation for 1789. From Romanticism to the present day, the arts, letters and thought in the western world have continued to reflect the ups and downs — crises and contradictions — which the ruling class imposes on the collective social body. The intellectual, and it makes no difference whether one is submissive or rebellious, remains trapped in the mesh of the system. Originality, the longing for originality, could be analysed in this light. But Josep Pla noted another motivation connected in part with the one I am discussing and already restricted to the actual mechanism of literary work in a true commercial context.

The reason is that, again since the beginning of the Renaissance, the profession of writer takes on a bourgeois nature. The invention of the printing press and the expansion of the reading minority altered the rules which govern the writing profession. The medieval man of letters, if he was rich, lived on his income and, if not, from the beneficence of a patron, appointment to the clergy or even Villon-style, more or less on the margins of the law, a tolerated vagabond. For a long time, we could say up to our own times, these forms of support of the intellectual still had and have a certain validity: well-to-do families continue to nourish their bookish offshoots; patronage adopts aseptic procedures of grants, subventions, travel or study scholarships, prizes; the appointment to the clergy is swapped for the university chair, journalism, editorial work; and bohemians, whether they be self-sacrificing or entertaining, have not disappeared from the scene. All the same, in spite of this the modern writer depends all the more, as times passes, on the public. He depends on an extensive and diffuse public which has access to his work through purchase and reading. And his income — or at least part of his income — and his prestige come from the sale and propagation of his books. There exists today a market for literature the like of which — either in volume or complexity — cannot be found in any previous cultural historical situation. The man of letters, like the businessman, has to think in terms of a clientele. And he is entrusted with the bourgeois ethic of the market. Plagiarism is then presented as an ignoble deception. Firstly, it tramples upon those laws mentioned by Pla which regulate a clean game and within the bounds of which writers ought to battle it out for the admiration and money of the customers. What is more, the plagiarist offers sophisticated merchandise. The purchaser acquires a certain book because it is by a certain author; he would be defrauded if the book were copied from someone else. And plagiarism is, above all, an act of theft: the plagiarist indecorously appropriates the intellectual goods of his neighbour.

The idea of plagiarism-theft makes an impression above all on the good will of the ignorant and the ingenuous. I wish to point out straight away that the literary phenomenon of plagiarism has only really affected the public and the critics when the plagiarist is a writer of high category. From time to time, some provincial or parochial rumpus is stirred up over plagiarisms perpetrated by mediocre journeymen; these are uninteresting incidents. The occasion is more exciting if the plagiarist is called Alighieri or Shakespeare, Stendhal or Virgil. Such discoveries as these have a morbid satisfaction; that produced through seeing some illustrious figures suddenly degraded. Rivals of the Roman poet found an agreeable opportunity to express their resentment in the hunt for the *furta virgiliana*; the resentment of the present-day literary dwarves sometimes searches for an outlet in similar operations of this sort. But that in itself should put us on our guard with regard to getting to the bottom of the problem. The disreputable pleasure which accompanies the denunciation of a case of plagiarism morally disqualifies the act from the start. And if it has been possible to accuse Dante and Shakespeare, Virgil and Stendhal — and so many others! — of plagiarism, and with good reason, does this not mean that plagiarism is less of a sin than we imagine it to be? Someone — a plagiarist, no doubt — once said that plagiarism is a robbery which is excused by murder; in other words, when the thief is so superior to his victim that the latter becomes nullified in literary terms. Our admiration for Shakespeare, the plagiarist, does not diminish; those he plagiarised are forgotten and perhaps justly: we only remember them because Shakespeare did them the honour of plagiarising them. In fact, we swallow many plagiarisms without realising it. And if we are to be frank, we cannot complain about it.

In spite of this, it is worth noting that, in certain periods, plagiarism was a permitted and hallowed intellectual custom. Each writer took what he considered to be the best from another, often literally in large passages, and inserted it into his own work in a totally natural process, without citing where it came from. Literary historians who detect these thefts tend to classify them modestly as borrowings. Specialists in medieval writings find an abundance of material for investigations by literary police. Plagiarism, it can be seen, has enjoyed if not general assent then at least the most respectable impunity in the past. Why should this be? It could be that at that time — the Middle Ages, for example — the writer was playing with an advantage: as a cultured man in a society less so than he, he had at his disposal certain texts which were unknown to his readers, so that he could in practice pull the wool over their eyes and offer as his own certain pages which came from another. It is very possible that this factor contributed to the exercise of plagiarism; this may well be so. But the plagiarist could not avoid the possibility that a colleague of his, as knowledgeable as himself in the texts of others, might prove it to be a flagrant copy. And if the plagiarist exposed himself to that risk, it is because he saw no shameful consequences to it. It would seem, then, that we should rather attribute this indifference towards plagiarism to other motives. The medieval writer worked driven either by vanity or by a desire for social efficacy; he wrote verse or composed books in order to win himself a little halo or to defend and disseminate a doctrine. The aim of his work was not — unlike today's author — to express himself; it was to create a work in such a way as to make it admirable or convincing to the public toward whom it was targeted. It is indisputable that, with this intention in mind, the plagiarism of another's work lacked any importance and even on occasion appeared to be advisable or necessary. Nobody considered that the ideas and words which made up a work were the property of the writer who had invented them. If a particular author had done it well it was not worth the effort to amend his page: it was enough to reproduce it exactly as it stood. "Je prends mon bien où je le trouve," said Rabelais. And the readers accepted it.

The modern preoccupation with originality could paradoxically provide an apology for plagiarism when it is seen from a particular angle. Pla believes that originality is "merely a form of pedantry and, at most, a momentary disorder". Perhaps neither pedantry nor disorder; but certainly a useless torture. The pretension not to resemble anybody else when it comes to writing or thought leads to failure right from the very beginning. The pessimistic and monotonous Ecclesiastes was not mistaken. Everything has already been said, everything has already been thought. Who is capable of writing an unpublished verse? The personal experience of each writer shows that even when he believes himself most certain of having attained an aesthetic or theoretic achievement exclusively by his own efforts, like Adam naming all things or Columbus discovering unknown continents, he is always in danger of coming across someone who has done it before him. It is not unheard of that a poet should one day discover, in his reading of an earlier poet, images, phrases, even complete lines, which he had written in total ignorance of the existence of the earlier work. There has been no plagiarism: it is simply coincidence. Such coincidences, which are very frequent particularly in the field of ideas, tend to be discouraging for those who suffer them; having considered yourself to be original, it turns out that you could be dubbed a plagiarist, even though plagiarism was impossible. There is no writer, however original, who could not be encumbered with precursors. It is an inevitable and fatal fact. And it should induce us to be more indulgent with deliberate plagiarism.

Objectively, we are not lacking in arguments to defend not only the justness but also the usefulness of plagiarism. One of them, the most serious, was that argued by Pla himself: anti-primacy. It is necessary to do what every cultured man who finds himself with a pen in his hand does: to continue, to carry on, to leave a small contribution in the stockpile of secure and ancient sensibility, in contrast with its social nucleus. The writer abandons any fickle and infantile ambition to invent gunpowder. As merely one more worker in the tradition of workers who encourage the growth of a theme within a literature, he takes upon himself the legacy of those who have preceded him and, with a happy and innocent modesty, limits himself to adding that which he can: his personal contribution of novelty. Minimal or extensive, this offering forms a sedimentary layer on the earlier gains and contributions. The man of letters to a certain extent re-writes that which has been written by his predecessors. To call it plagiarism is, then, excessive. He does not copy: he employs as literary material what others have positively put forward as their contribution. Someone will come after who will repeat the manoeuvre. If all has been done well, honestly done, nothing can be said, for cultural accumulation in itself is inevitably an effort of purification: a series of successive corrections. According to Pla, the primacy of the originals always borders on the superficial. And above all, it is necessary to continue; only continuity is profitable...

And, given that we are talking simply for the sake of talking, yet another ironic defence of plagiarism is feasible. There are many people who write. The public consumes a lot of literature and every day more providers of reading material are required. Obsessed with originality, the majority of writers strive to provide their readers with material which has been painfully carved out from their personality. On the whole, this production is utter nonsense. From a serious and utilitarian point of view, it is preferable to plagiarise sensible things than to write original rubbish. It would be better for the public to read profitable repetitions rather than unforeseen ineptitudes. André Gide, who was not inclined towards idiotic optimism, put it accurately: "Everything has been said; but since no one is listening it is necessary to repeat it." The tedious indifference of Ecclesiastes — *nihil novum sub sole* — is redeemed by this. It is necessary to repeat everything because no one is listening. Those naive writers who aspire to be original at all cost will be seen as nothing more than a counterproductive anecdote. A positive plagiarism is worth more than a superfluous original. One of the secrets of education is repetition; and if we attribute an activating and responsible function to literature we will not disdain this recourse.

The reply is easy to imagine. In order to plagiarise, to plagiarise well, one requires a lot of talent. Perhaps for this reason, as much as any other, plagiarism does not occur today on a large scale. Plagiarism at this level is an operation which is about as difficult as inventing — inventing well — by oneself. A special touch is needed to know how to choose a passage worthy of being plagiarised. Not everybody has it. Good plagiarism is only justified by its usefulness. It is obviously important to repeat; but it depends on what. I have always thought that the worst thing about plagiarism is not that it is a theft but that it can be superfluous. To be more specific: the worst thing about plagiarism is that it can be a redundancy without value. What is more, repetition will never be listened to if it is reduced to being a pure and limited repetition. A repetition is honourable and efficient when it not only reiterates an idea or a warning which has already been made but also reiterates it with new attractions which refresh it and restore it to a suggestive and fragrant splendour. The plagiarist has to hide the fact that he is plagiarising if he wants to be accepted by his readers.

No determined plagiarist confesses his plagiarism. Usually, when we take possession of alien concepts or words, we are quick to acknowledge our sources. The plagiarist avoids mention of his basic materials but, since he wants them to pass as his own, has to assimilate and amplify them so that the repetition can have its own peculiar attractiveness. And on this point, I believe, plagiarism and originality come together and are in agreement. The important thing about Stendhal's plagiarism is that the pieces plagiarised appear to be the authentic work of Stendhal. From the moment when Stendhal achieves the completion of the confusion the plagiarism appears reasonable. It is necessary to have the genius of a Stendhal, the intelligence of a Stendhal to make this work. No, it is not easy to plagiarise...

POLITICS

Charles Maurras says — or used to say — "Tout désespoir en politique est une sottise absolue". I apologise for quoting a wise old reactionary; but, if we are to believe St Thomas Aquinas, the truth of the Holy Spirit goes forth, whoever may pronounce it. That is all very well. On the other hand it should not be forgotten that if we are not active in politics it will be used against us. Finally, we should remember that politics is nothing more than the art of convincing our neighbour that he should be consistent with himself and with his dignity as a man. I leave it here for the reader's consideration.

PRIDE

The only pride which we find understandable is our own. I mean pride in the pejorative sense of the word. I don't believe there is anybody who is ingenuously or unconsciously proud. Overestimation of one's own worth, excessive self-regard, which are according to normal dictionaries what pride is, are rarely perceived as overestimation or as excessive. We know what we are worth and what we are; and we have no hesitation in thinking that we are worth *more*, that *we are more*. What in others strikes us as an unbearable obscenity seems quite acceptable in our own particular case. Why should this be? Perhaps because other people's pride makes us feel looked down on. Overestimation of one's own worth and excessive self-regard do not come about in a vacuum or in solitude; we apply them with reference to the next person. Like all vices and all virtues pride cannot be practised in isolation; rather it demands the presence of another person or other people to be directed against. The proud person is proud inasmuch as he asserts his superiority over those around him. Other people's superiority — real or fictitious — mortifies or irritates us. We need, on the other hand, to proclaim ourselves superior to our neighbours, quite often anyway. And it matters not whether it is one particular sort of superiority or another. We are not unaware that it is probably a falsely, or at least deliberately exaggerated, superiority. But we really need it. It helps us to keep going.

QUIXOTISM

Don Quixote is the hero who always comes out losing. This, in approximate terms, was the assessment of Cervantes's character once made by Eugeni d'Ors.[4] Ors, if I am not mistaken, was obviously aiming to contrast Don Quixote with Ulysses in order to draw a comparison which was flattering for the people of the Mediterranean. According to *Xènius*, Ulysses is the successful type whilst Don Quixote is the failure. The remark has a certain charm and undeniably is fairly accurate. I find, though, that it perhaps does not go far enough. It is not sufficient to affirm that Don Quixote is the protagonist of ineluctable reverses. Being defeated is a normal hazard, a frequent possibility, from which no one is immune, not even the most out-and-out hero — not even the most Mediterranean of them! There are all sorts of ways of being defeated. One can be overcome by a more powerful enemy, one can fall into an unexpected, lethal trap, one can destroy oneself in any stupid adventure, one can end up a victim of one's own disappointments or of one's own inhibitions: the result will be the same, granted, but the cause in each case is different. Don Quixote's failures ensue systematically from a strange defect which we might call optical if we did not know that it is mental: the knight of La Mancha is always misinterpreting what he sees; and so we must not be surprised if one disaster or another usually follows on. Don Quixote goes around with his eyes — or his head — infected with illusion: that being the surest way of getting things out of perspective, as they say. He doesn't see what is staring him in the face but rather something else that his imagination or will-power tells him is there. Cervantes had already notified us that his

128

man was as mad as a hatter and I suppose that present-day psychiatry has thoroughly studied and classified the illness afflicting poor Alonso Quijano. It would not even be worth talking about if it all boiled down to a simple clinical case, however outstanding the literary version of the tale. But there remains the fact that Don Quixote has become a symbol of universal validity and that Quixotism has a great standing as a virtue.

We must, then, review things just a little. Don Quixote's intention is invariably praiseworthy; it is not in vain that he devotes himself wholeheartedly to performing to the full his role as knight errant, righting wrongs and so on. The nobility of his aims could, occasionally, lead him to culpably misjudge his moment; at bottom Don Quixotes tend to be anarchistically irresponsible, as was demonstrated — by his own example, to boot — by Don Miguel de Unamuno in the commentary he wrote on Cervantes's book. But Don Quixote has, from the start, this one point in his favour: the wholesomeness of his aims. The drawbacks come later: Don Quixote is thoroughly mistaken as regards the most immediate reality about him. Where there are windmills he sees giants; where there are peaceful sheep he sees an aggressive multitude. He confuses a tavern with a castle and a barber's bowl with a helmet; he attacks the puppets of *maese* Pedro's show as though they were really Melisandra's assailants — he gets it wrong all the time. Failure is inevitable in each and every episode. Don Quixote stands outside reality and outside reality his bold valour is condemned to nothingness, sometimes sterile, sometimes ridiculous, always pointless. Is it also sublime as the book's line of apologists would have it? Perhaps so, sometimes: sublime with that particular sublimeness of the grandiose fiasco. But only sometimes. In general, the episodes of *Don Quixote* prove to be painful or funny rather than sublime. All attitudes and behaviour which we call quixotic partake of the same original failing. Every now and then we hear it in conversation: quixotry, quixotic are words in current use, there to be tagged on to people and actions that are strikingly of the here and now. And we are not dealing now with formally certifiable madmen, as was the literary case of Don Quixote, but rather with normal individuals.

Now the original defect is still there to be seen. These people — heroes in their own way, I have no doubt — come to nought like Don Quixote, charging at windmills and flocks of animals. What distorts their vision is identical in every case: twenty-four carat delusion. Discomfiture is never long in arriving, naturally: it can be taken as inevitable. Whenever we hear someone's quixotic spirit being positively appraised, we ought to be immediately on guard. There are no two ways about it: a Quixote is simply and radically a monstrosity. Ors, in his comparison, evoked the classical image of Ulysses: cleverness incarnate. Ulysses is the very opposite of Don Quixote, precisely because cleverness is likewise the very opposite of blind enthusiasm, of lyricism and of candour. Don Quixote, Don Quixotes in general, lose sight of the real world; Ulysses is the perfect realist, a shrewd tactician who can never overlook the tiniest detail of the world about him. Ulysses' ideals are of an obviously homespun mediocrity; and thus he will always be, in the eyes of refined people, a less radiant hero than Don Quixote. Ulysses clearly does not have a heroic vocation whilst Don Quixote does. Ulysses is a hero *malgré lui*, deep down, whereas Don Quixote, on the other hand, lives out his obsessions with the models of novelesque chivalry that he wishes to imitate. Ulysses is a committed husband, ordinary in the extreme, who feels nostalgia for his own home, his good lady and the firesmoke of the home country. His adventures, big and small, befall him because of the changeable humours of the gods or because of life's ups and downs. But his ultimate goal, over which he has no control or sway, is placid, conjugal and domestic stability.

Alonso Quijano is deranged by fantastic, improbable things he reads about in books; literature poisons him. After taking in a thousand tales of knights errant, he determines to behave like them and to outdo them in glory and fame. If Ulysses' adventures are fortuitous, Don Quixote's tend to be deliberate: I mean Don Quixote goes in search of them, unlike Ulysses, who is just impatient to reach Ithaca. Don Quixote goes in search of adventures on account of an indigestible over-consumption of literature. Quixotism is always an infected outgrowth of literature. If you ever have the misfortune to encounter someone fancying himself as a Quixote, you can be quite sure what his game is. The selflessness that we regularly ascribe to Quixotism is pure literature. Perhaps it is not phoney; but it is an unreal selflessness. The Don Quixote in question loses sight of the real world. He comes a cropper. This, though, is not what the trouble is. The trouble is that he enjoys failure: he finds a sort of inner satisfaction in it. This is because the imitation Quixote comes *after* Don Quixote, and he believes that his degree of failure measures the extent of his proximity to the Cervantine model. Literary subtlety becomes more and more precisely detailed. And after all, Quixotes are no use for anything. They are a bunch of useless whiners, showing how far imbecility can stretch.

READING

I know nothing about it, but I feel there must be a certain kind of neurosis characterised precisely by our present-day fearfulness. I say it must be a neurosis — a complex, or something like that — because, in all honesty, the facts of the matter allow for no other explanation; at least not so far as I can see. It's quite another problem to investigate whether or not this fear of being sucked under by the everyday whirlpool of surprises and tragedies is justified from any angle. Maybe we're faced with a disease typical of our age, or (at any event) a disease of ages like ours, when the essential certainties of a society lead to breakdown. Be that as it may, we must mention that there's a clear trend towards escape, evasion, which is aimed at fleeing from the inimical face of immediate reality.

This occurs, for instance, in reading. It also occurs in other kinds of activity, in all of them; but here I'm just concerned with reading. There are many people, among them those we often refer to as highbrow, who shun any contact with new books. Any author, any work which has not stood the test of time is rejected with virtuoso extravagance. And should any exception be made to this practice it's bound to be in favour of something innocuous, delicate, historical: in short, something out of date. Which of us has not met, in indefinite numbers, the kind of gentleman — inevitably present at any get-together — who contemptuously takes refuge in the classics? On another level, but still within the same category, there are people who don't read newspapers; they're disturbed by the bustle of topical events which demand a committed response: they prefer to daydream, and are in their element with an account of Wamba or Napoleon's mothers-in-law.

And it's odd how once they start talking they never stop. The anachronistic reader employs undoubtedly wide-ranging points to justify himself. These will doubtless relate to the fabled dimensions of the cultural legacy to which we, of course, have fallen heir, which demands our attention with the peremptory *ars longa, vita brevis* taken in a very strange way. They will go on to say that a proper understanding of the present can only be achieved through a prior understanding of the past. Lastly they will add that a classic is, naturally, a tried and tested commodity underwritten by the consensus of centuries whereas contemporary writings are subject to the permanent danger of mis-representation. Think of all those writers, famous for a few years, who have vanished into deepest oblivion. Moreover, the history of today can only have light shed on it from the perspective of yesterday...

Yes. That's all true. But it's not the whole truth. I would even venture to state that the reverse is more true. Because, when it comes down to it, the person who reads (and lives) now isn't an abstract entity, cut off from time — from their own time — and likely to yield, inevitably, to the vague temptation of becoming a statue. If culture, understood as a legacy and the classics, sanctified as an indisputable asset, still have any meaning this stems, in short, from their continued presence among those things we regard as valid and alive. After all, we can all differentiate easily between what is archaeology and what isn't. A literary work from five, ten, twenty or more centuries ago can retain its appeal more or less undiminished and this saves it from being branded as an antique. A classic isn't a classic because it's old but because it's still modern, up-to-date. When a present-day reader picks it up in search of refuge, this is a bad sign for the supposed classic because maybe it isn't genuinely so; or a bad sign for the reader who can only take pleasure in its outer casing, in its anecdotal or trivial trappings.

Reading isn't an escape. Even if many people read only to seek an acceptable substitute for drugs, reading is the complete opposite of getting drunk or befuddled. One reads to understand oneself, to understand other people, to understand the age we live in. And even to understand the past, which is ultimately also our past, today's past. We turn to works of literature in search of new or better information, opinions, courage, regarding the world around us, the world we form part of. And anything other than this is a waste of time; that is, a waste of *our time*.

However, we ought just for a moment to stifle this tendency towards advice or anathema. Let us, here too, attempt to understand above all. The most cursory glance tells us that we don't all require the same things from literature. We can essentially discern two basic types of readers: basic and extreme. The first type seeks in a book — a creative work, naturally; poetry, short stories, a novel — a journey round the world of the great human fantasies. The second group wants to attain a more subtle, more precise understanding of the world about them through the book and its author. There also exist professional readers, who read from vocation or duty; the critics or literary historians who, although they actually fall into one of the other two categories, are embarked upon a different adventure which frequently obliterates the naive feeling of spontaneous enthusiasm felt by the ordinary reader.

I hasten to add that both the reader who aspires to escape, or the specialist, and the reader seeking a better view of reality share a prior factor, something which is undoubtedly the mainspring of the normal mechanics of reading literature. In this they differ, above all, from the reader we have described as professional. And this something is the element of play, of pleasure, even of superfluity contained in the act of reading. One reads precisely for relaxation, for amusement. Reading books appears amidst the routine round of our daily obligations like a soothing pause, a breathing space when we can recover our energy prior to plunging back in again.

There is, then, a first movement of pleasure characterised with special features by the usual attributes of aesthetic enjoyment. But literature diverges from the so-called fine arts in that it always has a logical content — if I may use this term, which I do with the utmost reserve — and makes constant reference to human affairs at their most explicit. Literature cannot fade away into a display of sheer formalism neither can it be reduced to an exclusively technical value. Music, so they say, is an abstract art — an architecture of sound; the plastic arts can, simply and without damaging their essential nature, leave behind all meaning. But poetry and the novel live off people; they are linked to them, they must sing or tell tales of them: sing or tell tales of their ambitions or problems. So, at the same time as they are faced with the aesthetic phenomenon in itself, the readers become involved with — and commit themselves to — that shred of humanity which the book offers them.

This is where the system of preferences to which I referred in making the initial distinction comes into play. For, given that reading is recreation — the unpunished vice of Larbaud — every reader will structure what they read around their own moral or psychological needs. Some — and here I'm over-simplifying again — will try to find a substitute for dreams in literature; others, a substitute for life. Some will seek to escape, by means of a book, from the painful urgency with which life assails them; others will demand a wider contact with the inevitable, voracious, tempting bitterness of this life. We should, however, make yet another clarification. Both readers, both kinds of reader are, in my opinion, by the very fact of being readers, presupposing a distance between themselves and life. The people who *live*, who live to the full — or think they do — feel no desire to read. Theoretically, *vital* people feel this desire no more than any healthy animal such as a cow: they are the healthy animals. But such people do not exist: people are always sick animals. And if they don't seek a cure — or a sedative — in reading, they will do so in other means that we usually think of as degrading: alcohol, the cinema, whatever.

In any case, however paradoxical it may seem, the substitute for dreams and the substitute for life I referred to do not meet their respective shortfalls. It would be natural for the realistic among us to take to reading escapist literature and for the absent-minded, fearful of reality, to turn to books which would inform on the matter. But in general this compensation doesn't work like that. We see, instead, that every reader carries on following the thread of their normal worries in their reading. The person who fears street life does so in books: our disgust doesn't agree to disappear just because its object appears in a literary context. At the same time, love for things and for people, in all its fatal tragedy, emerges just as clearly in the preferences of the reader. When all is said and done, reading is pursuing life, and everyone does this in their own fashion.

REGRET

Some reason or other can always be found — providing you look for it, of course — to regret anything, even the most noble act you have ever done. Nevertheless, regretting something achieves nothing.

SAVAGES

It seems that, throughout history, instances of refined civilisation, opulent urbanity, structural beauty, have had as a counterpoint an over-evaluation of the *natural* life. The over-evaluation being made, of course, by the refined and the urbane. Horace's *Beatus ille* sets the mark and the whole thing goes from strength to strength. A more or less sincerely-felt fatigue resulting from exacerbated metropolitan mysticism arouses nostalgia for those amiable freedoms, simplicity and healthy rural customs. This nostalgia is predominantly literary. It is writers who — to use a typical cliché and I regret the only one I can think of is in Castilian — postulate all that "menosprecio de corte y alabanza de aldea."[5] In all likelihood, however, it was not merely a literary twitch. When European society achieved the delicate and rational life style of the French eighteenth century — the epoch most far removed from pre-history, according to Ors — the most sophisticated and sensitive souls distinguished themselves by their penchant for the blessed folk who lived in the natural state. Marie-Antoinette and her ladies often lost themselves in pastoral comfort in the royal parks. Courtly poets joined in with this, manufacturing standard bucolic verses. Philosophers pondered the delights of a world uncontaminated by conventions and problems of etiquette. Ethnographic curiosity was focused on far-off lands which had barely emerged from a dark association with instinct and basics. The *bon sauvage* was thus converted into a myth symmetrical to that of la *bergerie*. Rousseau and his ideological heirs propagated this through an accredited literary output and bequeathed it to posterity with a rather decorous moral reference. It is easy to explain this nostalgia for an innocent society — or non-society — of pristine and virginal openness, immediate contact with zoology and unmystified botany, for those who spend their life in the rarified atmosphere of the court or the big city. Weariness with civilisation is no mere rhetorical coquetry. Moreover, civilised people tend to feel ill at ease at being just that — civilised.

It would be superfluous to point out that the above-mentioned penchant for the environs — the countryside, the exotic land of the savage — of civilisation sprang from a false basis. The idea that the courtier, the city gent, respected the peasant or the aborigine was ridiculously absurd. In the eighteenth century peasants and shepherds for whom the ladies of Versailles yearned, lived a most precarious existence — hunger, exploitation, illness, discomfort, fear, vexation were their daily bread. It would be the American or African *bons sauvages* who, complete with a ring in their nose or the scantiest of cover for their decency, were gloriously sculpted in the engravings in European books. Colonialism had not as yet entered its most extensive predatory and afflictive stage. There is, however, every reason to believe that those marginalised fellows, free from the enslavement offered by civilisation, had a pretty hard time of it. These days, now that we can look at this from a clearer perspective, we are amazed at the ingenuous devotion which some people in the eighteenth century dedicated to savages. We even begin to suspect that the panegyrists of man in a presumed natural state might well be hypocrites or simpletons. Today's newspaper reader who gets news from Angola, South Africa, the Congo, would never believe that the *bons sauvages* of two centuries ago were happier than those of the present. Happier, more admirable or more enviable. Among the root misery and cannibalism which still endured, the *sauvage* could hardly be *bon*. The Romantics prolonged the Rousseaunian illusion. Later, colonial empires and their companies, created for the exploitation of colonial natural resources — and men — diverted to

some extent the literary propensity of savage-loving sentimentality. The majority of writers from the golden age of
colonialism left the *bons sauvages* to one side and wrote
symbolist poems, intellectual novels, travelogues like
those of Paul Morand, treatises on the concept of anguish
or being and time. It couldn't have been any other way. In
the meantime, the image of the *bon sauvage* was not
erased completely from the routines of the average European. The vision held by the white man — middle or working class — of the colonial world, came from Kipling,
Tagore and their like; and from the innumerable publish-
ers of strip cartoons which took as their theme the picturesque topography and humanity of submissive peoples
and subjects.

Nowadays, however, all this has suffered an ironic
reversal. It has turned out that, suddenly, savages — the
real savages from different parts of the globe — have
resolved to live like the civilised. This decision has caused
bitter surprise among the populations which can boast
refrigerators and professors of philosophy. This surprise,
it should be said in passing, does not constitute full-
blooded disappointment. It is not that our citizens are
shocked to see the savages' aspiration to abandon their
theoretically privileged condition of savage. The surprise
comes from certain other considerations. For example, the
bon sauvage has become aggressive; in other words, he's
no longer *bon*. The net result is that the classic cliché of
the singing, hard-working nigger, the Hindu sage, adorer
of sacred cows, the respectful, ceremonious Chinee, the
fatalist, sibylline Moor, has been the object of a complete
overhaul. The facts themselves have brought this about.
The *bon sauvage* had been a resigned savage, servile,
peaceful, eminently useful. But now this resigned, peace-
loving and useful savage has taken up arms, embraced
nationalism, developed a consciousness of social rebellion
and obliges his overlords — the great-grandchildren of the
inventors of the notion of *bon sauvage* — to defend themselves — and colonialism. Colonialism, being a business

139

concern, will not be easy to eradicate but is, at the moment, on the defensive. European and non-European in the same boat feel that the good savage has become a bad savage. Civilised man is now keen to declare and avow, in an unexpectedly energetic fashion, the intangible superiority of civilisation — with the monopoly of civilisation for himself. Of course this was already predicted by certain prophets. Let us remember that a whole anti-liberal tendency in European thought distrusted entirely the myth of the *bon sauvage*. Their representatives are already quick to point out, I told you so!

The truth of the matter is that this is not really justified. The *bon sauvage* trick was a false imputation, as I have insinuated. However, the myth of a bad savage promoted by news agencies, important columnists and salaried sociologists is a further false imputation as considerable, if not more so, than its precedent. Civilised man does not realise that certain aspects of his savageology are completely reversible. When a European smiles at the picturesque presentation of a tribal witch doctor or an equatorial king with tattoos, paint, bones, rings; or when we scoff at ponchos, fezzes or turbans, we should stop for a moment to think that the embroidery, trimmings and emblems of our chiefs are no less grotesque, if considered coldly. I hardly find any difference between one type of regalia and the other; and what I say about the sartorial elegance of the dignitaries could be repeated about other aspects of the question. Naturally, the savage, good or bad, lives through penury and hardship which situate him on the lowest of levels in a suburban sphere with regards to his civilised counterpart; it is for this reason that he continues to be a savage. This hardship and penury has been imposed upon him by civilisation, or colonialism. As such, it would be obscene to condemn him for deficiencies for which he is not responsible, for deficiencies which we, the bearers of civilisation, have inflicted upon him.

Moreover, the savage — even the worst savage — has clearly shown himself relatively inoffensive. From time to time, newspapers tell us of macabre events perpetrated by the natives of jungle and desert: cannibalism, rape, pillage, hunting of the white man, martyring of missionaries. Western sensitivity is scandalised by the primitive crudeness of the methods employed. It has no right to go any further. Quantitatively speaking, the criminal attempts of savages bear no comparison with the results achieved by civilised man in the same sphere. Were we able to calculate the effect of wartime excesses perpetrated by the white man over the past hundred years, we would find this all too discouragingly clear to see. From Napoleon to Hitler and Hiroshima, millions of deaths through violence, absurd systematic destructions, insatiable oppressions fill the pages of the history of civilised countries. The bloodiest of tribal apotheoses unleashed by the totality of savages during the same period are nothing but placid games of chess in comparison with the horrors attributable to the advanced nations. With one further detail: the savages have never read Kant, nor do they quote Goethe in their intimate conversations, nor say that they adore Wagner or Debussy. Civilised man most certainly does read, quote and absolutely adore these and every other monument of this finely-honed culture. It is also he who wins hands down at the end of the day in matters of appalling massacres, larceny, abusive insults to the civilisation he created. If it is only for the reason that it is he who has the nuclear bombs, invents the gas chambers or creates concentration camps, whereas the good savage (or bad savage) must resign himself, on the other hand, to his paleolithic spear... or the rifles he has been sold by this self same civilised man.

SCEPTICISM

I should like to write an apology for Scepticism. The following are certain topics which would need to be made plain therein:

141

1. *The Intellectual Aspect.* Sceptics are always and by definition, reasoned and reasonable people. They cautiously put themselves on the side of reason and, accordingly, are usually right. In other words, they doubt and are right to do so.

2. *The Moral Aspect.* Scepticism is the only viable corrective for fanaticism or dilly-dallying. It is the only one: there is no other. Moreover, sceptics tend to practice sarcasm, which is — as everyone knows — a hygienic and efficient form of charity.

3. *The Social Aspect.* Sceptics will never be assassins. Nor will they ever commit the sin of heroism. These are two virtues which should be valued in their own right.

4. *The Political Aspect.* Revolutions are certainly never made by sceptics. They sometimes prepare them and often purify them. Nothing more. On the other hand, they never induce their fellow men to hatred, resignation or indifference.

5. *The Technical Aspect.* Sceptics — and only sceptics — are sensitive to time, history, the concrete and unrepeatable. They are, therefore, at the antipodes of any tendency towards abstraction.

6. *The Literary Aspect.* Scepticism is incompatible with lyric poetry, oratory — whether sacred or profane — and metaphysics. If sceptics try to write verse it will turn out pedestrian and acidic. If they try to make speeches they will stutter through indecision or scruples. If they try to compose treatises on being they will end up satirising them.

SERVILITY
There is no such thing as disinterested servility.

SEX
Sex is not a serious subject, whether of conversation or of
literature. This, it seems, has been the general conviction
for centuries; and it still lives on today in extensive regions
of societies we know. In literature, love certainly used to
be taken seriously — and how! — but not sex. Poets, novelists and dramatists, even fairly recently, have only been
able to view sex through witticism, jokiness or grotesque
exaggeration. Either they have shut it out or pretended it
didn't exist, submissively respecting established taboos, or
else they have brought it up under a light that was preva-
lently comic. The classics of the genre bear me out in this
regard, be they Martial or Pietro Aretino, Aristophanes or
Rabelais. The exceptions are so few and far between that
at this moment, without stopping to think, I could only
mention one: the Marquis de Sade. But sex in de Sade is
an almost ominous presence, never more than that, a con-
fusedly diabolical pretence in which human reality, physiological and psychological, is subordinated to an
instrumental role as insult to the Divinity or to a certain
ethical sanctimony. Apart from de Sade, then, the prevail-
ing attitude is unanimous: sex becomes — *qua sex* — the
object of systematic laughter-making, whenever writers
admit it to their ken. Medical men and moralists are, of
course, another matter; sex for them has a purely physical
or social significance and it is partly depersonalised. Likewise in everyday exchanges, we have to make this technical exception concerning those who deal with sex neutrally
and with professional discretion. Beyond this, indeed, one
finds only the dirty joke, sarcastic innuendo, smutty gossip; anything for a laugh. It is as though man were incapable of talking about sex except in terms of obscenity, and
as though obscenity were somehow or other inseparable
from ridiculousness.

> Qu'a faict l'action genitale aux hommes, si naturelle, si
> necessaire et si juste, pour n'en oser parler sans vergogne
> et pour l'exclurre des propos serieux et reglez? Nous
> prononçons hardiment: tuer, desrober, trahir; et cela,
> nous n'oserions qu'entre les dents?

Old Montaigne — one of those moralists who have written
on sex with conspicuous seriousness — was half right: he
was right to the extent that his questions point out the
tendency to evade frank and normal discussion of the subject. On the other hand, he was wrong to see this as having to do with the sense of shame, for example. Shame has
often been a direct influence on people's behaviour. But it
is also true that precocious language and literature have
always irresistibly permeated the behaviour of western
society. The point is that we are talking about *shameless*
language and literature. And predilection for such verbal
activity has, in all ages, reached sizeable proportions
which the guardians of public morality have wished, in
vain, to repress. Pornographic writing has had to be clandestine, and the jokes are told *sotto voce*; none of this has,
however, prevented their abundantly accumulative diffusion. Furthermore, tolerance of this kind of thing is generally more lenient than strait-laced official declarations
— everywhere — would have one believe. Nowadays, most
states can point to their own severe legislation against
extreme manifestations of oral or printed libertinage. In
practice, what impresses is the leniency with which it is
applied. There are entertainments, like music-hall and
theatrical review, that in many countries thrive on good-
natured but unequivocal ribaldry relayed with coarse
gusto; and publications of a similar tone circulate without
too many obstacles. As for the habits of conversation, no
comment is necessary; everybody's individual experience
tells the whole story.

This experience, moreover, also confirms that the tendency to witticisms about the lower abdominal regions is
not by any means exclusive to particular social classes or

particular peoples. Perhaps what we call upbringing, proper upbringing, together with certain religious influences have ensured that, in recent times and in certain clearly defined social milieux, the dirty joke has been frozen out. Victorian puritanism and its consequences, spun out to the present day in one part or another of British society, would be one example of this. But this type of repression is always relative. Prudishness, wherever it is to be found, never manages completely to cast out the taste for licentious humour. And if the folklore of any particular community is full of it then cultivated minorities have no qualms about joining in, whole-heartedly. Lewd or racy literature is far from being the exclusive domain of the masses. The *Ragionamenti* were published with the sophisticated reader in mind; and Rabelais's texts expressly appeal to a humanist readership, the only one capable of picking up the puns and the sardonic, succulently erudite flourishes of *Gargantua* and *Panatagruel*. The printing presses of the eighteenth century put out a prodigious quantity of blue books, which were bought and read by the high bourgeois and the aristocrats. Beyond the bounds of western civilisation — outside Europe — things must have gone along similar lines. I could not vouch for this, but there is good reason to believe it so. Ethnologists, the investigators of tribal vestiges in colonised territories, relate that among natives of those lands it is not unusual for direct allusions to sex to be greeted with rowdy, spontaneous hilarity. The effect is universal.

Before continuing it will be appropriate to record here another exception, which is difficult to match with conventional literary registers — literature in the strict sense — but which is not at all detached from the main literary trunk. I refer to that kind of text which, alluding to a famous specimen, we can label as the *ars amandi*. They were authentic manuals of erotology. Some of eastern origin, more or less genuine, have come down to us. Montaigne evoked, in one passage in his *Essais*, a series of significant titles of lost works which he recalled in his

145

methodical intellectual memory:

> De quel sense estroit le livre du philosophe Strato, *De la conjonction charnelle?* Et de quoy trattoit Theophraste en ceux qu'il intitula, l'un *L'Amoureux*, l'autre *De l'Amour?* De quoy Aristipus au sien *Des antiennes delices?. . .* Et le livre *De l'Amoureux* de Demetrius Phalereus; et *Clinias ou l'Amoureux forcé* de Heraclides Ponticus? Et d'Antisthenes celuy *De faire les enfants ou Des nopces*, et l'autre *Du Maistre ou De l'Amant?* Et d'Aristo celuy *Des exercices amoureux?* De Cleanthes, un *De l'Amour*, l'autre *De l'art d'aymer?* Les *Dialogues amoureux* de Spherus? Et la fable de *Jupiter et Junus* de Chrysippus, eshontée au delà de toute souffrance, et ses cinquante *Epistres*, si lascives?

Lascivious they were not, all of these works — going by the reports of them which survive — giving us to believe that they avoided the titters. They constituted a didactic genre, designed to enhance carnal pleasure. Their hedonistic intention implied a step beyond the idea of sex as a subject for laughter. Ovid, who does survive, disappoints us slightly because in his *Ars amandi* sex, despite being the protagonist, is there in stylised and elliptical form. If the texts mentioned by Montaigne were more explicit and direct, they would have constituted a first effort to endow sex with seriousness.

It does seem, however, that the tendency to be instructive in erotic matters soon gave way to pornography. Pornography has been produced in varying degrees, needless to say, in all ages and in all places; still, there is no doubt that at the close of pagan antiquity it took over from that modest tradition of erotology. The norms of voluptuousness become replaced by mere titillation, and this is not now so much the excitement *to* voluptuousness as excitement *of* the sexual imagination. An *ars amandi* was an invitation to indulge in the delights of the flesh; a pornographic tale is nothing of the sort. The aim of pornography is to foster sexual anticipation in a person's obsessions or illusions. It is quite significant that pornography's more receptive public is made up of adolescents or of adults with difficulties in the normal attainment of sexual fulfilment: in other words, generally speaking, people who are sexually inactive or inadequate. For them pornography is a substitute and a sort of mental or imaginative onanism. Now the basic procedure of pornography is description and this description has to be spelled out in strikingly graphic terms. The literary predicament of pornography is that it lacks an appropriate vocabulary. A pornographic story can only be told in everyday language; its whole suggestive, provocative, power would be lost if the choice were made to describe parts of the body and actions with the neutral terminology of official dictionaries. A pornographic text would lose all or virtually all its attractions if it used words like vulva or copulation. The trouble is that the only alternative to this quasi-scientific lexis is slang and euphemism. It is in this way that the comic element is re-introduced into the treatment — the pornographic treatment now — of sex. Pornography is very often ridiculous because its vocabulary is ridiculous.

We can see this in the *Raggionamenti*, or in the *Soneti lussuriosi*. Pietro Aretino, divine Aretinus, the dyed-in-the-wool humanist who wrote distinguished theological and pious speculations, owes his prominent fame only to his scabrous dialogues and poems. Their merit is not to be denied. Even today, four centuries on, those pages are still occasionally put out in secretive and much sought-after reprints. The disinterested reader, in other words the one who takes up the *Raggionamenti* and the *Sonetti* out of purely cultural curiosity and not in pursuit of libidinous excitement, discovers that these literary pieces of Aretino are written in terms of an all-pervading grotesqueness. It is certainly true that the *Raggionamenti* conform to a satirical aim. But nobody could deny their titillating charm. This is even more true of the *Sonetti*, which aspire to nothing else. Since their suggestiveness is sought at the level of a racy directness, on a plane of intimate connivance with the reader, the author is reduced to having recourse to the most colloquial modes of diction. Coarseness, then, is the result. Aretino is certainly suggestive and he also makes one laugh. His appeal is to a reader who is responsive to pornography; he provokes laughter in this and in any other reader. I know of no work of pornography, of unabashed pornography, that completely escapes this generalisation. There are certain books that dwell with lingering intensity on the sensual, without ever abandoning an urbane formality of language; what they are is pseudo-pornography. Leaving them to one side, the affirmation holds good: when pornography is committed to words, it must be resigned to expressions with camp overtones. Reactions to pornography, even among the most naive, are also ambiguous: excitement is never just excitement: it is customarily accompanied by guffaws or smirks.

We observe that love in literature — literature about what we call love — is at least partly a defence against man's proclivity to view sexuality through the optic of the grotesque. Sex is present there; it has an essential role. For the lovers, the act of love-making (this itself a highly symptomatic formula) represents the carnal consummation of mutual devotion and, consequently, a most respectable occurrence at the opposite pole from the grotesque. A whole literature with uplifting and spiritual pretensions fomented by love has the impulse to redeem sex from moral depreciation. It does not succeed in this, however, and it is limited to drawing a veil over sex itself. This is why it is prudish to do everything to hush up the lovers' final, confidential bedroom scene or to clothe it — remember the delicate scene in *Romeo and Juliet* — in an ennobling phraseology. Not to beat about the bush: love always appears — is presented — before or after coitus: never in or during coitus. The ultimate physiological encounter will be cautiously avoided. It is the way to avoid grotesqueness. Pornography, on the other hand, specialises in intercourse and in preparations for intercourse. Pornography, moreover, eliminates love — elevated sentiment — and concentrates exclusively on fornication. Its protagonists are rarely lovers: pornographers are great respecters of love. The characters in obscene adventures are chance partners, without emotional bonds, seeking in their encounter the simple — or complicated — fulfilment of desire. Crude representation of copulation, the innermost details of the secret moment, were they to be revealed about genuine lovers, would degrade the supreme image of the man-woman relationship. This, it seems, is a very deeply rooted prejudice. Pornography steers well clear of this area. It operates from preference upon figures who are divested of truth to human life. Fornicating puppets: these are the creatures that pornography habitually portrays.

There is one reason which explains this comic understanding — or misunderstanding — of sex. And it is this: description of the sex act, whether one likes it or not, entails the reduction of humans — man and woman — to a complex of attitudes which can only be seen as animal; and people will always laugh at themselves when they see themselves behaving like beasts. Humanity has a high opinion of itself *as a species*. Humanity, in our estimation, constitutes a pleasant exception within the zoological world: the human is the animal who is no longer an animal. All the philosophies and all the ethical systems that we have so far come up with insist upon this point. The effort to stifle or to spirit away the beast that humanity continues to be, an unceasing and inspired effort, certainly confirms humanity's exceptional condition within nature. Even so, it is an effort which will never succeed in suppressing — forgive the truism — our basic animality. The body and its demands constitute an indisputable fact which no amount of spiritualising illusion can get round. Elemental physiological necessities, arising every day, cropping up at every instant, insist on being satisfied. This unchanging impertinence is offensive to us and disqualifies and belies that high and mighty image we have forged of ourselves. This is why physiology, in most of its manifestations, has received repressive treatment: the constant endeavour has been to cover it up since no feasible alternative was available.

Physiology corresponds to low functions. To perform them humans withdraw, go away, hide. Only eating has escaped this restriction and, even so, there are on record accounts of societies and of people which have been particularly sensitive on this score and have consigned it also to the discreet darkness of small back rooms. All of the body's other natural activities which we consider incompatible with our glorious superiority are the object, to varying extents, of one or other form of socially imposed squeamishness: sneezing or spitting, scratching or shitting, belching or coughing. It is not only dainty deference towards those around us that determines the precautions insisted upon by politeness when we have to perform one of these actions; such precautions are likewise gestures by which we try to gloss over or conceal the insolent expansions of our bodies. Sexual behaviour has always been subjected to the most drastic confinement to shadowy seclusion. Some very specific prejudices weigh down upon sex, of course; but it is ultimately the area of our bodily comportment that seems most closely identified with animality. A couple in the act of trying to reproduce themselves — as someone put it — is, for the traditional mind, the authentic, the inadmissible stock image of the beast caught in the supreme moment of zoological embodiment.

Lechery *in actu* can cause a decidedly depressing impression as a spectacle witnessed or evoked, whether it involves oneself or someone else. Leonardo da Vinci affirmed that the act of love-making — sex fully expounded — is so ugly that "la natura si perderebbe", nature would run to extinction if the fornicators could see themselves in action. He was exaggerating; the perpetuation of the species is in no danger in this regard. The problem, though, is not to do with ugliness — or is not so much to do with ugliness — as with that other matter, the animality that rears its head. We, as humans, those special beings, made in God's image, the claimants to so many virtues, creators of arts and philosophies, the favourite

children of fate, suddenly renounce all those high-sounding qualities and abandon ourselves to fleshly fun and
games, like a dog or a fly. Individuals cannot see themselves fornicating and are blinded by their own pleasure.
But they can be seen by others who know that they fornicate — and how they fornicate. It is the sexual function
itself, torn from its *human* context, that is seen —
whether it be with the eyes or in the imagination. And it
is the contrast that creates the laughter; it is *comical*. It is
comical to think of this anti-animal that the human being
would strive to be reduced to the most animal of actions.
All the bombast of human convictions is hereupon
deflated: humanity becomes grotesque in humanity's eyes.
Pornography makes the most of this. The coarseness of
sexual terminology — the slang and euphemisms alluded
to earlier originates here: we cannot have serious names
for things that are very far from serious. And if a hint of
perversion or irregularity happens to become involved, the
comical element is increased: the human being behaves in
this case not just like an animal but even like an aberrant
one. Jokes about homosexuals are all the more hilarious
precisely because of the animal extravagance of pederasty.
Rustic stories based on accounts of bestiality — the shep-
herd having it away with his goat, and so forth — are
another source of great amusement. Humans are always
prepared to laugh about sex, come what may; prepared,
then, to laugh about themselves.

I just said 'the most animal of actions'. Objectively, the
expression is false. The physiological quality of sex is no
more — or less — animal than any other animal bodily
function. But the fact is that, for us, for the so-called
civilised person, the sexual act is held to be more vile —
vile is the right word — than any other occupation of a
physiological order, including the excrementary. This is
possibly due to the aspect of relative luxury pertaining to
sex. Urinating or eating are indispensable acts, neglected
at our mortal peril; belching or sneezing are more or less
inevitable actions. But the sexual instinct, in this beast we

151

call human, is subject to exceptional control. If chastity is a virtue, it's because the option is there for humanity. To this extent, then, sexual practice is something we choose, or not, to engage in. That is to say: the facet of animality represented in sex has every appearance of being something deliberate. Humans, in fornication, behave like animals, return to the animal state, *because they choose to*. We behave ridiculously in the full knowledge of doing so. In one of his books Josep Pla quotes a sentence of Lord Chesterfield on where sex puts us. I know nothing at all about Lord Chesterfield, so I must rely on Pla in calling him to witness. "The pleasure is momentary; the cost is exorbitant; the position is ridiculous", wrote the British nobleman to his son. The position is ridiculous. Is it really? We shall not go here and now into elucidating the scope of meaning that the word ridiculous covers, or ought properly to cover. Whether the *position* is ridiculous or not, looking at things from another galaxy, there is no doubt that, in practice, everyone — everyone who, at some moment or other is ridiculous because they can't avoid it — is convinced of the ridiculousness of the situation. "This is how we have found it and this is how we shall leave it", is Pla's comment. But this does not alter one jot the circumstance described, does not take one jot away from the *ridiculousness* itself. And one simply laughs about it. What is comical about sex is painfully obvious.

I consider that this motivation is decisive in the problem we are addressing. Not the whole story, evidently. Sexual jokes have also been interpreted as a sign of rebelliousness: as small outbursts of subversion against established morality. Jokes of this kind are directed, irreverently, at the abstract myth of wholesomeness built into all societies. Society, any society, through its very existence, favours regulation — rules and regulations — and is its guarantor, particularly in matters of sex. And it fosters prejudices and conventions that ensure regulation is accepted as natural. It must be so, if society is to survive, if it is to be sustained with a minimum of internal coherence. The fervent supporters of virtue are quite right when they point to aspects of collective depravity as something akin to the mortal dissolution of society itself. Peoples, human groups, invariably attain solidarity at the expense of sacrifices made by their component individuals: the sacrifice of dissipating or stagnating tendencies. Individuals must work, be sober and honest, risk their lives if necessary for their country, keep their word; they must sacrifice their understandable inclination towards idleness, towards debauchery and deceit, towards cowardice. In the sexual domain, citizens must adjust to norms which ensure public order and the normality of juridical relationships. Under so many pressures, individuals tend to resign themselves to conformity. But not without internal stress. And their response comes out in the form of humour. They joke about everything that society forces upon them as something sacred, something prescriptive and to be respected absolutely. This is revenge. They rebel through words, without bloodshed. In the aspect of sex, social pressure is intense; and so correspondingly strong is the temptation to joke about it. All of this is obvious and it explains one of the causes behind the comic conception of the subject of sex. Even so, the important thing is what we remarked on earlier: the comical nature of sex is something intrinsic, because it arises from the contrast of two antithetical notions about humanity, the sublime and the bestial.

We may believe that this contrast has been made sharper by Christianity. Christians add to their purely natural patents of nobility the stamp of being a temple of the Holy Spirit. St Paul goes on at length about it in his epistles. Nowadays — I mean within the epoch of Christianity — the fornicator is not merely that singular phenomenon of nature, magnificent and illustrious, that is humanity but someone who is that and, with a bonus of dignity, a temple of the Holy Spirit. And the idea of this temple sullied in fornication was bound to be a staggering concept. The encouragement of purity, and consequently a lugubrious disdain for the body and its weaknesses, the denial of the animal in us, was a necessary corollary of this. Sex is denounced as something filthy, as perhaps the most denigrating of all the filth that might menace us. "Formatus de spurcissimo spermate", according to one mediaeval pope talking about man. Sex is unclean, most decidedly: disgustingly dirty. But the need for procreation is there; and also there is the need for a *remedium concupiscentiae*: matrimony will satisfy both. This is as high as sex can go in the estimation of the church. Only inside matrimony — the lesser evil — is it redeemed. "Better to be married than to be roasted in Hell," St Paul specifies. All in all, better not to be married, if chastity could be maintained. Anything else is sinfulness, blemish, ignominy. It is within Christendom that, probably in reaction to this, the most virulent pornography has been produced. In any event, the Christian view, promoting humanity to a supernatural status in the hierarchy of creation, was bound to add further comedy to the fundamental comedy of sex. The beast is pronounced now to be not just a plain and simple human being — such as provoked the mockery of Aristophanes and Martial — but one who is, moreover (as we've said), a temple of the Holy Spirit. The moralist was alarmed at humanity's fall, reproving them for it and, portentously, reacting to it with severe gestures of fussy disapproval. The masses, less portentously, found in it nothing more than a supplementary cause for guffaws — or smirks. Pornographers derive the benefit from this situation. Aretino is more disgusting and more hilarious than his pagan counterparts precisely because he stands upon an extraordinarily substantial base of theology. And it is theology which makes the pornography of Aretino and of so many other Christians, so cuttingly funny.

A digression: the background of Christianity in sexual matters makes comprehensible some episodes in western eroticism which would otherwise make little sense. For example Don Juan, or de Sade, as I have already suggested in passing. Don Juans, like sadists, are rather more than pathological specimens. The rapid, unpredictable, treacherous polygamy of Don Juan and the pleasure seasoned with cruelty of de Sade are perhaps deviant but natural forms of biological behaviour. Dr Marañón attempted to explain it in the case of Don Juan and no doubt some other physician, psychiatrist or endocrinologist has done the same for sadism.[6] Both types, then, the Don Juans and the sadists, would be biologically possible in any society at any time. Nonetheless, Don Juan and de Sade stand out in our literary canon because the sexual peculiarity of each of them has a religious — or anti-religious — aspect which only Christianity could have given them. Sex, in Don Juan and in de Sade, becomes unexpectedly blasphemous. Each of them brandishes his sex against God, the God of prohibitions, against the repressive and demanding Spirit. Libertinism in the Japester of Seville and in the eighteenth-century marquis is not a search for dissolute pleasure but an insult to the Divinity; and just because it is an insult to God, blasphemy, it acquires a marked degree of seriousness. Detached from Christianity, Don Juan and de Sade would lose their dramatic force and would be figures of fun. They would have been figures of fun in the age of Pericles; and they will be figures of fun a hundred years from now. At the present, they can scarcely appear to us as mere clinical cases. When God is dead, Don Juan and de Sade vanish, leaving nothing more than a picturesque residue. Under Christianity, on the other hand, they have achieved a diabolical dimension. If ordinary copulation is funny, the exasperated copulations of Don Juan and de Sade provoke wonder or terror: animal Man at last rises to the challenge and makes of his animality an element of provocation.

When Romanticism was exhausted, when the nineteenth century grasped hold of science as the only means of salvation and positivist ideology spread, sex began to be considered from another point of view. Only *began* to be; the rectification still has a long way to go and was to begin

155

with a timid attempt, slow and difficult. Even more difficult, maybe, than it would have been at any other time, because Romanticism had overemphasised the spiritual complexion of the amorous bond. The Romantics are responsible for vast quantities of poems and novels of a fantastically false twilight languor or of an ardent and extravagant pathos, where erotic realities are as obsessive as they are sophisticated. Strictly speaking, it must be admitted that the first attempts at the serious recuperation of sex had taken place in the eighteenth century, in France, through rationalist philosophers and especially the *libertins*. It was then — de Sade himself said it, unless my source is mistaken — that there were people who thought that "ce qu'il y avait de bon dans l'amour n'était que le physique". Voltaire, expounding his view of love, is more specific, "il faut ici recourir au physique; c'est l'étoffe de la nature que l'imagination a brodée". Some of the most representative works of eighteenth-century France, among them *Les Liaisons dangereuses*, are in this category. But here we still find imagination doing its embroidery, leading to pornography and consequently laughter. The *libertins* initiated a change. If the ideological potential and direction which that tendency introduced had continued, progress would have been more rapid. It was not to be. As the little-known but admirable Arrigo Cajumi said, the nineteenth century *betrayed* the eighteenth. Romanticism, in this as in many respects, was a step backwards. Only when Romanticism was pushed aside could sex be looked at again without disgust and without imagination.

Albert Thibaudet pointed to Emile Zola's *La Terre* as the first attempt to bring sex into literature on a serious level. It matters not whether it was Zola or someone else; the change of direction was promoted simultaneously by many factors of various kinds which converged on the second half of the nineteenth century and which are pre-eminently present in our own times. I will not say the transition was sudden or total; it could not be then, nor is it even now. The derogatory attitude to sex has endured.

Pornography, even literary pornography — I could mention, as a well-known example, the name of Guillaume Apollinaire — continues to maintain its prestige and its audience, or even to increase them. The sublimating approach is not in decline either. There is also, to confuse matters, an occasional recrudescence of sexual hatred, of eccentric Catharism, such as we find in Tolstoy's *Kreuzer Sonata*, something rather unusual in earlier centuries except in the outlook of professional ascetics. But the attempt to treat sex seriously has been made; it grows and spreads. The interventions of medicine and psychoanalysis become important in due course. Contemporary society has finally recognised that humans — men and women — are not asexual beings; and that the sexual organs are a part of the body as worthy of attention and care as the stomach or the eyes. Despite the pseudo-scientific character of manuals of sex instruction, of conjugal education or of sexual hygiene and of works of popular psychology, there is no doubt that this sort of work has helped to dispel many anxieties and to restore to sex a sense of cleanness and openness, without titillation or squalor. The physical today is connected not so much with the old idea of animality as with the idea of health. And it is not funny any more, or not so funny as it was.

Progress has been hard-won and painful. European society, strait-laced as ever, hypocritically strait-laced and in certain sectors maybe more hypocritically strait-laced than ever, has resisted it. The nineteenth century rallied to the watchword of liberalism, and particularly to the most representative of its freedoms, freedom of expression, of the press. It was by relying on this freedom that the serious restoration of sex in literature was to be, or should have been, achieved. The judicial history of the last century demonstrates that the liberalism invoked at that time was an empty ideal when it came to sexuality. The intent was waylaid or obstructed by reaction. Even without having mentioned sex directly, Flaubert and Baudelaire and some others found themselves before the courts

157

on charges of outraging public decency. It was an easy and convenient accusation, and one which was to be repeated from time to time in the twentieth century, despite the indisputable retreat of official prudery and despite the no less indisputable progress — via the cinema and light reading — of sexual pragmatism. There are a few spectacular cases which should be recalled. James Joyce's *Ulysses* and D.H. Lawrence's *Lady Chatterley's Lover*, two essential novels of our times, suffered vicious persecution from the guardians of morality. Vladimir Nabokov's *Lolita* is one of the last scandals of this kind, as far as I know. And Henry Miller, with his *Tropics*, *Nexus*, etc., has beaten all the records of banning and censorship. The list could be extended. And not all the repression has been judicial or administrative. There are other kinds of social pressures, tenuous but insidious, which impose an irksome, caution on the writer. A book as basically harmless as *Si le grain ne meurt* by André Gide was subject, barely forty years ago, to a prudent dilation; in 1920 it was published in an edition of only twelve copies, without the publisher's name, and in 1921 in another edition of only thirteen more. In 1925 there followed two expurgated edition and only in 1928, or so I understand, did Gallimard publish the book commercially. All the above is a matter of reluctance to be overcome, the last gasps of puritanism on the retreat. But it can still not be ignored.

Zola and the Naturalists, when they got interested in sex, did so in some degree so as to carry forward in this area too their fight against Romantic exaltation. They were aiming in some ways at a demystification of love; or of what was called love by the Romantics, prolonging a centuries-old literary tradition. Not that the Naturalists were the first to attempt it, certainly. Baudelaire had written earlier an outspoken and apt phrase, "De fait, nous ne pouvons faire l'amour qu'avec des organes excrémentiels." It was an assertion of simple directness. But Baudelaire, a poet, and a Christian poet at that — one hundred per cent Catholic — spoilt it at once by bringing in the concept of original sin — or of sin *tout court* — which so attracted him personally. Naturalism, having no theological axe to grind when it rediscovered sex, remained on the plane of material reality. It found itself suddenly dealing with a force that in the life of the individual and of society proves as powerful as money, or more so. Sex, then, was no laughing matter, as indeed money was not. Erotic experience is set in its proper place; a natural physiological occurrence, not glorious, but not unclean: with no sentimentality, either positive or negative. In fact it was the Naturalists, accused of preferring in their books the most sordid aspects of life, who brought sex out of the abyss of sordidness to which it had always been consigned. If their descriptions of sexual themes have a sordid side that comes not from sex in itself but from the state of social degradation in which sex is encompassed. That very sordidness, identified as a stain and a disgrace, contains the seed of an implicit claim on behalf of sex, on behalf of the re-exaltation of sex. The conflicts which surround it are moral and economic; sex is the victim of them. That is the premise at least.

In the gradual rehabilitation of sex it is not only literature that is involved, of course. It is reflected and exemplified by literature and, for that reason, we must pay attention to it. But the tendency is a complex one and a wide variety of circumstances combine to further it. The participation of philosophy, of currents of thought in general, was decisive. An ideological trend originating in the eighteenth century, more or less obscured during the Romantic era, aimed to overthrow established conventions. Other critiques of various origins were added, coinciding in their hostility to the inflexible and stuffy morality of the past. Scientism became an ally. A facet of this offensive was the retreat of Christian influence in the intellectual sphere where the dispassionate recognition of sex began. Science in the narrower sense was a part of it if only in that it contributed a concern for prophylaxis. The danger of venereal disease, once medically understood, turned against the vulgar stereotype of sex. And there was Freud, right or wrong, leaving a profound impression on the mentality of the average individual. The collapse of the ancient moral tenets by which the western peoples lived took place, moreover, in the midst of an unprecedented economic and social upheaval. Or perhaps this upheaval is one of the factors which caused it. I mean industrialisation with all its consequences from the aggressive rise of the proletariat to the conformity of easier living favoured by technology and credit. The communications media — or mass media as it is known — promote a relative relaxation of moral restraints. In barely a hundred years, the changes have been prodigious. With respect to sex these changes have been enormous, rational and effective, in a liberating direction.

Like so many other social processes, this is one of evident ambivalence. On the one hand, it has given rise to a surprising amount of trivialisation of sex. In ceasing to be sinful sex ceases to be shameful and shaming and imposes itself wholeheartedly. It functions as a bait for stupendous commercial exploitation. Nowadays in some countries sexual exhibitionism is practised with elegant and agreeable *sang froid*. The screen and magazine pages have commandeered the bodies of exceptionally attractive young women, who now have no secret from the masses. Marilyn Monroe, Brigitte Bardot, Sophia Loren have generously let themselves be admired. The cinema has often made the bed the scene of titillating sequences; I am not speaking of blue films, murky and unsavoury, but of films for public showing with pretensions to art or to pure entertainment. The erotic adventures of princesses and actors, various forms of *ballet rose*, capture the attention of the readers of the world's press. Practices — who could qualify them now as good or bad? — have become elastic; and the scope allotted to sexual freedom is everywhere a generous one. In the average citizen of advanced countries there is an area of behaviour and conscience which swings between a sugary sentimentality with Romantic antecedents and a fever of eroticism, freed finally from impediments and restraints. Love, when it survives in accordance with the classical prescriptions of feeling, does not conceal or exclude sex but accepts and incorporates it. It cannot be said that all this is yet another transformation of that ever-present trend to licence which we can trace through history. There has always been an element of dissolute vitality in people's daily lives, under the surface of theoretical morality and feigned virtue. But it was a throbbing which was indecent, disapproved of, imprudent. Famously licentious periods like the Italian Renaissance did not forget the blameworthy nature of their licence. Nowadays it all takes place with no remorse, with few moral preoccupations, and with no fear. Sex, cleansed of ancestral apprehensions is now something obvious and, like everything obvious, it becomes trivial.

On the other hand, there is now also a serious return to these very issues, a new and austere way of reconsidering them which literature — literature of a certain kind — picks up and makes explicit. Sometimes the appearances are bewildering, bewildering that is for the unprepared reader who despite everything remains immersed in Puritan survivals, or who only escapes from them into the surrounding climate of trivialisation of sex. The bewilderment rises from suddenly finding oneself confronted with sex presented with thoroughgoing objectivity. The reader feels inclined to dismiss it as pornographic. Novels like those of Henry Miller — *Tropic of Cancer*, *Tropic of Capricorn* — seem at first like a limitless outpouring of obscenities at the level of dirty postcards of the kind kept under the counter in red-light districts. The accumulation of salacious detail, deliberate and obsessive, does recall the methods of the pornographers. But that is not what it is. The unashamed depiction of sex in Miller and in many other present-day writers has a purpose which goes beyond the enervating *frisson* produced in the suspicious reader. The goal is sincerity. Sex is a part of life, turbulent or serene, mechanical or magical, indisputable in its capacity to disturb physically and psychologically. An account of the human race which tried to suppress all mention of sex or tried to falsify it would be an inaccurate one. Both pornography and the lyrical — Platonic, Romantic — version of love were false to humanity in being false to sex. In the past honest sex had to be sought outside literature, in private documents like Samuel Pepys's diary. It is only nowadays (and nowadays dates back a while) that writers have taken up the theme with equanimity. The paroxysms of Miller and others do not contradict this account of the phenomenon. Alongside grotesque sex and disguised sex there is now plain sex.

Throughout the present note I have mentioned in passing certain representative names of great literary prestige which I do not need to insist on. That of André Gide, for instance. Gide's autobiographical papers display a persistent sexual passion, which in his case takes on an aspect of self-justification, that of a homosexual provocatively asserting his right to pleasure. Proust, Peyrefitte and Genet in their different ways deal with the same subject, and Carlo Coccioli — in *Fabrizio Lupo* — does so within a Catholic framework. D.H. Lawrence made a broad case for sexual fulfilment, for a kind of vitalism centred on sex, which achieves moments of vigorous, expressive richness. The case of James Joyce in *Ulysses* is more complex: sex — the flesh and the weariness of the flesh — appears there in the fullness of its exaltation, diverse in contradiction to conventional morality and obsessive in the subconscious stream, the interior monologue, of our secret thoughts. Miller and Nabokov, whether in respect of normality or of perversion, are simply chroniclers of sexual behaviour in modern society, objective and concise in their writing, relentless to the smallest detail. There are also those like Alberto Moravia or, on another level, those like Françoise Sagan who are producers of books in which the erotic has a considerable emphasis, and can be labelled as popular — popular, that is, on the level of the unclassifiable literate populous of our times. We could include Huxley and Mann as well.

162

Aldous Huxley will not take time on the depiction of juicy situations; but in *Point, Counterpoint* and *Chrome Yellow* he analyses and judges the reality of love with dazzling neutrality and detachment, with an entomologist's frightening, dispassionate curiosity. There is a page of Thomas Mann in his *Magic Mountain* — for which he should be mentioned if for nothing else — and which is, as Marius Verdaguer said, a song to the immortal beauty of organic matter, and which is at the same time a naked observation of sexual inevitability as seen through manuals of anatomy and physiology. The outlooks of these authors are quite diverse and the scandalous content is quite varied too. The fact is that, as a result, sex in its literary version is no longer either grotesque or stimulating. It is just sex — an inevitable aspect of human nature.

The overwhelming concern with sex in certain writers contrasts with the scarcity or even with the total absence of the theme in others. Love occupies rather a modest place in the novels of quite a few major writers of the twentieth century, as I have remarked elsewhere in this book. For Hemingway, for Kafka, for Malraux, for Sholokhov, for Camus or Pratolini, for Sartre or Ehrenburg, sex has not the sentimental iridescence we observed in Flaubert, in Stendhal — or in Paul Bourget or Gabriele d'Annunzio. In them sex, *de-sentimentalised*, isn't ever present in the way it is in the works of Joyce, Lawrence or Miller. It is kept within bounds in its rightful place, the place that corresponded to it once it had been *de-sinned*. The true substance of that literature is metaphysical, social or political. Sex, therefore, retreats from the foreground of the novel; it is not there, either sublimated or displayed. But neither is it forgotten altogether. When it is appropriate to place it on the scene to give a more *complete* picture of humanity, the author mentions it. But then again it is just sex, that demystified sex which modern society practises, no more than that. The actions and reflections of the characters are not centred on their genitals; they have other things to do and think about. They copulate like everybody else, normal or abnormal. They just do not make this activity a major issue whether with the psychological pretext of love, or with that obsessive preoccupation with the "world of fucking" (to quote Henry Miller) which the others display. It is the counterpart of the trivialisation of sex that we observe in all current forms of society. Sex is *important*, as nutrition is, but not more so. Nor less, for that matter. If it does take on the role of a problem, it is in the context of social conflict or medical diagnosis. Frustrated or satisfied, sex does not go beyond clearly defined boundaries. Frustrated or satisfied, sex is related solely to the urge of physical satisfaction or to the fulfilment of a physical and psychological relationship between a man and a woman. We come upon the notion of hedonism again.

Hedonism. We cannot ignore the word. Detached from any transcendental implications sex becomes serious — neither comical nor lyrical. Serious, divorced from the joke or the poem. So its natural emergence must take place strictly autonomously, if I can put it like that. This is confirmed by a significant fact: not since pagan times has there been such an abundance of *Art of Love* books as there is now. All those works which we previously evoked in a passage of Montaigne have their multifarious modern versions, with persuasive titles, written by physicians or whoever, who attempt to supply the nubile public with technical information aimed at increasing the completeness of carnal pleasure. I suspect that from the Graeco-Roman period — I mean in the western world — to the present age, few text-books of this kind were written. Nowadays there is an extraordinary quantity of them. Guidebooks to sexual behaviour have multiplied. Often they are directed purely towards conjugal relations, aiming at sensual and moral well-being in marriage. But the lessons are applicable in situations not approved by the law or by the church. Sex itself benefits from them. Sex thus confirms its seriousness. Perhaps if the world continues on this path there will come a day when jokes about sex will be inconceivable, except in extreme cases. Perhaps we already have the right to hope that sex will not even admit irony. Pornography will lose all its delectable efficacy. The seriousness of sex would be a good thing. It would be a good idea if we could match it to gastronomic seriousness, for example. Life would be less dramatic and less stupid — less repulsive and less ridiculous...

SILENCE
Often, in fact almost always, to remain silent is *also* to lie.

STUPIDITY
The precept, or advice, given by the Catechism, if I remember it directly, said or says, "Suffer patiently your neighbours failings." The eighteenth-century philosopher, however, more mundane and caustic, offers a more particular version of the theme which is not unsuggestive if considered carefully. "Pardonnons-nous réciproquement nos sottises" he writes, "c'est la première loi de la nature." To tell the truth, I couldn't really say whether it could be described as the first law of nature. The recommendation, however, is not without substance to say the least — let us forgive each other our stupidity... The skilful redirection to which the ecclesiastical notion has been subjected is quite striking. For a start, the failings for which indulgence is requested are reduced to one woundingly concrete term: stupidity. And from a fairly rigorous moral point of view, couldn't we affirm that all human weakness is, in essence, stupidity, pure and simple? Specialists in the subject would say yes. On the other hand, our bewigged citizen — *nec nominatur* — whom I quote, was still more precise with his reflexive pronoun, as to the extent of his admonition each other. Forgiveness must, in effect, be mutual, and it is there which we must forgive: our acts of stupidity and respective inanity.

In fact, when the philosopher said *sottise*, he meant silliness, stupidity, daftness, simplicity, in the most basic and correct meaning of the words. He used as illustrations examples which are not really pertinent here. I believe we would not be digressing too far from his intention if we made a few generalisations of our own. Realistically speaking, few defects in our neighbours annoy us more than one in particular — crassness. It is annoying not just for ourselves but for the neighbour in question. Everyday existence forces us to *put up with*, forgive and tolerate our neighbour's words and deeds: his short-temperedness, filth, insolence, temerity and coarseness. To forgive him, in such circumstances, merely means overcoming our irritation, disaffection, or the discomfort that his offence produces. In the last instance, our forgiveness comes to afford us a certain self-satisfying inner relief. It's a completely different story when stupidity is involved. Other people's stupidity offends us, obviously, but it also instills in us a harsh disdain for the responsible party and that is bad. We may forgive him for his stupidity, for the offence which his simplicity has inflicted. It is not so easy, on the other hand, to repress our disdain; and to disdain our neighbour is, at least for me, a rather distasteful, or at any rate unpleasant operation.

The basic thing, and let us not forget this, is that it is a question of forgiving each other our stupidity. The commandment smarts like a piece of sarcasm. For is there anyone brave enough to admit that they commit acts of folly? I don't mean to say that the exception never arises when, overwhelmed by the evidence against us, we don't have to admit contritely that one of our own slips falls into the insulting category of stupidity. Only God knows how much it grieves us to have to accept it. Our pride is, more often than not, monstrously invulnerable; and above all invulnerable in the face of our own private stupidity. However, though we may come to admit it, nothing is so mortifying as to have this judged by others. We know from experience, from the experience of other people's stupidity, that it is in this case our attitude, our folly, that has aroused our neighbour's disdain. And if it is always uncomfortable to disdain another then to be disdained by others is more painful still. The philosopher's malice may well have been directed at this insight. A good dose of modesty, in this as in everything else, would be an excellent ethical purifier. When all is said and done — and here we parody the Latin American poet — who is there among us who is not stupid at times if not always? The rest is literature.

If a laudable percentage of the world's electoral registers practised mutual forgiveness when confronted with stupidity then all would be a lot better. Let us not deceive ourselves about this; although appearances may lead us to believe that the worst evils of humanity come from the sphere of crime, hatred and ambition, there is nothing more certain than that crassness and its consequences are as much, if not more, to blame. And just as much as — or instead of — forgiveness we should suggest *forgetting*: "let us forget one another's stupidity." As long as we go on not forgetting it we will have nothing but disdain for each other, with all its terrible consequences. The spectacle of human folly — our own and other people's, everybody's — is inevitable; we will have to ensure that it is rendered if not totally innocuous, then as harmless as it can possibly be. Perhaps that would be the equivalent of proposing, as a general rule of conduct, too heroic a form of stoicism. I don't know. But the catalogue of sacred virtues should include this one; without name or transcendent reward, but so intimately satisfying, healthy, and so ironically defined by that distinguished thinker of the eighteenth century... Voltaire, who else!

7

TEMPERANCE

'Moderation, moderation...' This is the advice of sensible people and we have heard it many times; but it is also some kind of diffuse legal precept, distilled in the current codes and in the norms of urbanity. The whole of society preaches and demands moderation. Those who are rebellious, passionate or impatient, whether in body or in spirit, think this to be pure hypocrisy: infectious *Tartuffisme*. All attacks on bourgeois morality, when uttered in the name of a hypothetically sacred freedom of life and instincts, agree against this one idea: against moderation. In it they have wished to find the typical caution of the bourgeois, the greyness and mediocrity of the bourgeois raised to the category of an ethical imperative. This is the inspiration for the literary rebellions of *fils á papa* which the bourgeoisie has to suffer repeatedly; such is the case of the *poètes maudits* at the end of the nineteenth century; of the surrealists in the twenties, of the little-beards of Saint-Germain-des-Près; or the beat generation, or the angry young men of more recent times.

However, the thing does not appear to me as simple as that. The *ne quid nimis* is a principle — a conviction and a postulate — much older than the present class structure and too constant in the moral systems of all times and all countries for it to be rejected so easily. Look at this carefully: the faults condemned by all moralities are always the same. Approximately, they are the seven deadly sins of the Christian doctrine: anger, lust, gluttony, sloth, pride, greed, envy. The differences between alternative moral systems are minimal. They relate to particular cases so that one will make more allowances and another less. But, in substance, the fixation and definition of the most

168

serious vices is identical. This is what should be under-lined: the mediaeval Christian, the pagan stoic, the orien-tal sage, the modern rationalist, when defending a morality, all agree on its contents.

This unanimous agreement might induce us to think, as the theologians would like it, that there exists one natural law, an innate ethical system, inscribed in human nature and previous to any positive religion or any philosophical system. I do not believe in it much, if at all. Common sense, on the other hand, can explain the fact from a dif-ferent perspective, somehow down-to-earth but with bet-ter guarantees of reaching some understanding. Those sorts of behaviour qualified as vices or sins are rejected precisely because they are antisocial. Antisocial, or anti-economical: it is all the same. And they are antisocial not against this or that historical form of society but rather against any society: they were antisocial in the ancient and feudal societies, they are antisocial in the modern bour-geois society, and they would be — indeed they are antiso-cial — in a socialist society. Antisocial because they are anti–economical, in fact. If we analysed the seven deadly sins one after the other we would understand this easily. Those seven tumultuous passions — let's insist that they need to be taken as such, as *disordinate passions* — when projected onto individuals in any way which is absorbing, annihilate them as economic agents. We do not need to explain what would happen if, momentarily, our neigh-bourhood abandoned itself massively and wholeheartedly to the wanton cultivation of unrestrained concupiscence; society — life in common, any kind of life in common — would suddenly become impossible.

But we do not really need to go to the extent of carica-ture. Every vicious individual, every sinner, is individually an anti-economical element and, in consequence, antiso-cial. Vice frustrates them in their quality of social being: it dissipates them. This already happens in the private sphere, and moralists — everywhere — usually tell stories with enchanting examples according to which the way of

169

sin can only lead to ruin; to the ruin of the soul, but also to the ruin of the body and of the state. It is not unusual for reality to come down on the side of these moralists. But even if that is not the case, even when the debauchee gets away with both health and pocket unaffected, society inevitably resents the loss of economic energy involved in his actions. This is why society tries to defend itself against the dangers of vices. The law does not punish sins in their current manifestations.

However, a fair number of criminal acts are immediately related to them. Envy is not penalised by states but slander or theft is; anger is not, but injury or assassination is. Lust is not penalised but then rape or corruption of the youth is. And what *criminal* actions would the vicious individual not fall into in order to satisfy vice and its voluptuous demands? And besides the public sanctions, there are others even more dense and complicated: the conventional ones, applied by society on its own. The vicious individual is the object of quarantines, boycotts, spite, insults. Are these motivated by an urge for virtue amongst the non-vicious? This is what the non-vicious believe. Deep down, however, they obey a spontaneous movement of social self-defence. Vice, sin, is a germ of disintegration. It dissolves and deletes. It undermines the economic foundations of society. For this reason it is necessary to drown it; for this reason it is necessary to repress or to mediate those who practice it. Puritanism is more of a political or police attitude than a specifically ethical one. Tolerance towards vice, which often occurs in fairly puritanical climates, does not contradict what I am saying; it results from the fact that vice, in certain circumstances and if properly controlled, can offer good benefits; and in such cases people turn a blind eye.

In any case, it is equally necessary to consider that the frontiers of vice are never clear-cut. From the perspective of society, the essence of sin has nothing to do with the violation of a divine or moral law abstractly established upon humanity. Rather, it is a single lack of moderation. Sins are disordered passions. And where does disorder begin? This is a delicate question. Those kinds of behaviour catalogued in the list of deadly sins are not reputed as sinful if they take place within certain limits. Moreover, insofar as they do not go beyond such limits, such problematical but indistinct limits, they are in fact favourable and profitable conducts for the smooth progress of society. They are so profitable and favourable that, without them, society would fall into chaos and poverty. Society would not want to extirpate them.

Let's not be deceived by appearances: society does not stand for virtue either — not for a dry and indomitable virtue. As much as vice, society fears virtue. While vices are anathema, society does not want to spread diametrically opposed altitudes: it does not aspire to exchange anger for patience, lust for chastity, pride for humility. This other extreme is also anti-economical, antisocial. If all were saints, society would fall apart as fast as if all were methodically vicious. An excess of vice would lead to chaos but an excess of virtue would lead to languor. A society full of virtuous people — radically virtuous, saints — would get stuck in a wretched simplicity, held up by asceticism and renunciations.

Certainly society does not forbid sanctity as it tends to forbid vice but it does not encourage it either; it simply allows moralists to preach virtue, because it needs to be coherent with its own prejudices. It is not at all obvious that society would still tolerate such moralists if ever virtue obtained a striking success. It would probably put up as many obstacles as there are nowadays against the propaganda of vice. But society knows too well that virtue — extreme virtue — has little attraction and that consequently there is no risk on this side. Society has no interest in abolishing what can be described as the raw material for sins. These passions, if kept in order, are the great power-engine of the economy, of any economy. Pride is noxious; self-love and the desire to excel are, on the other hand, efficient forces in stimulating people towards pro-

171

jects and accomplishments of a positive kind. Lust destroys families and spreads incoherence in customs; a frantic continence would be no better and, in fact, the perpetuation of the species and some modest sensual fantasies are guaranteed by habits and peoples. Gluttony is depressing, unfortunate, embarrassing; a measured hedonism — at the table and elsewhere — always has more advantages than a harsh sobriety, even more wholesome advantages. Anger provokes painful acts of violence; a certain amount of vehemence, of excitable susceptibility, is an excellent incentive for the effort of the individual within the community. Sloth is deadly; an aspiration to a comfortable leisure, on the contrary, produces lovely cultural fruits and stirs work. Greed offers a sinister facade; saving and provision, even if unaccompanied by selfish intentions, are collectively useful tendencies.

Furthermore, several projections of sins, always in the scale admitted by society, favour industry and trade or at least some industries and not a few trades. In a civilisation like ours (and I have no doubt that, despite differences, the same also happened in other times), the keenness of both married and single ladies to embellish themselves in order to be liked by men, the taste for refined meals and delicate drinks, the distractions with which one has to fill empty leisure time, all these serve to promote fortunate economic expansions. The pity is that people, more often than not short of cash, do not have more time for them. Society does support these non-virtuous, but equally non-vicious, kinds of behaviour. Society assents to the dissertations of the moralists, schematic and radical as they are; however, it practises a different kind of virtue. The usual virtue has nothing to do with the ethical systems of theologians and philosophers; it is a mere and pragmatic middle term: *in medio...* — yes, moderation — temperance, in the good sense of the word. This is all. Horace's verses are full of recipes with this one wise intention.

All in all, whatever the society in which people have to live is like — ancient, feudal, bourgeois, socialist — the important thing is to keep doing the best possible job; which is to keep going, both individual and society, together. Moderation is a criterion of conduct proved to be right... I have nothing to say against it. Simply, I would like to make it clear that a little amount of excess, from time to time, will not be too pernicious. And I think it is fair that everyone can choose, in committing excesses, the vice or virtue one prefers. Excesses — real excesses, let us not deceive ourselves — are the only things that brighten up life.

THOUGHT
Take note: every thought is a bad thought.

TIME
While you sleep your beard grows: this is time.

TO BE
We all imagine ourselves to be different from what we are. Were this not the case, we would not have the patience to put up with ourselves.

UXORCIDE

Uxorcide is, ultimately, a consequence of marriage; in the same way as adultery or divorce is. I do not believe it is possible to deny this. I say consequence not because marriage is its necessary condition but rather because uxorcide *is provoked by it*.

VENGEANCE

Vengeance, if I may put it this way, comes later. Max Scheler made it very clear in *Ressentiment*. The immediate reply to an offence is not yet an act of vengeance. The person who receives a punch and immediately returns it without prior thought is not taking revenge. What is more, in our everyday vocabulary and within our system of values, this prompt and countervailing reaction, directed against any type of affront, is not normally given the name of vengeance. An exchange of blows or insults is simply a quarrel. However, not everyone is strong enough or indeed brave enough to take the risks involved in a quarrel, even if it is only verbal; humans tend to be prudent animals and try not to become mixed up in difficulties without a minimum of guarantees. When the contest is between contenders of equal force, the fight goes ahead there and then. Those able, or believing themselves able, to face up to their opponents on equal terms will not hesitate to resort to the subsequent offensive, either by word or deed. Vengeance, on the other hand, is the recourse of the weak.

The strong resist aggression *sur place*; the weak wait until they cease to be weak to pay back the ignominy suffered. It is this postponement which gives life to vengeance. It gives it first by definition; in other words, because vengeance always presupposes a period of pause between the offence and the redress for the offence. But what is more, this period of waiting gives the vengeful attitude a very concrete and special psychological aspect. We can believe that the instinctive punch with which we repay a previous affront is a gesture free from malice, a kind of reflex action and, as such, clean and gentlemanly. Where vengeance is concerned, by contrast, the offended person has been brooding on the memory of the insult during the whole period of time leading up to the outburst. The blow of the avenger is characterised as being a malicious blow.

When I say that the weak wait until they are no longer weak to take their vengeance, I am not saying that they necessarily have to be strong at the time of avenging themselves. Quite often the act of vengeance is cunning, crafty and insidious. It continues in its realisation to be an act of the impotent. However, the impotent attempt an act of retaliation when they find themselves with an opportunity or some other particular advantage. The advantage, in effect, could be an increase in strength: by chance, by training, by means of a trick or through perseverance, the weak and oppressed may become powerful and dominant and will make use of the favourable circumstance in order to punish the ones who wounded them in their lowest hour. The advantage could also be of another kind, any other kind. Impunity, for example. An assured and resentful weak person is one of the most fearsome beasts in natural history. The occasion will then result in the decline of the enemy: the offender, previously arrogant, is now weaker than the weak one — although the latter has not ceased to be such — and the weak one revels in the situation.

It is unnecessary to point out that vengeance is one of those words which is laden with negative ethical repercussions. History and literature clearly contain cases of illustrious vengeance, horrifying vengeful episodes which are, however, adorned by the lofty prestige of honour, friendship or patriotism. In any case, generally, vengeance is not frequently linked to nobility and high ideals. This is a handicap which the physically or economically weak possess: they never appear to be noble, at least not in the eyes of the strong. The small, sour act of vengeance, hardened in its meanness which forms part of the everyday relations between people always gives the sad impression of malice. And it is curious that, if we examine it well, the mechanism of human action which we call vengeance is, in the end, no better or worse than any other. Everything depends on the level of its utility. Think, for example, of that diffuse form of vengeance which constitutes collective rebellion. The uprising of a people or a social class which has suffered oppression or injustice is vengeance. Would we say that it was *ignoble*?

VICE

There is nothing like poetry, like good poetry of course to consecrate any obvious foolishness under the pompous aspect of an incontrovertible truth for many centuries to come. A few chance words can put ideas into the heads of generations of ingenuous readers, so much that the enchanted formulation tends to distract from the idea behind it. In the language of our neighbours Jorge Manrique left to posterity a couple of brief definitive lines which, through being repeated and disseminated, have gone on virtually to achieve the value of strict paroemiology, as if they had come forth from the anonymous mouth of the people, from tradition. Although it seems almost unnecessary to quote them, they are:

> cualquiera tiempo pasado
> fue mejor.[7]

I believe it is unnecessary to clear the poet of responsibility. Manrique warned that such was nuestro parescer (our opinion) in particular circumstances, and the context of the *Coplas* gives them precision. However, in general, when someone brings up the aforementioned brief lines, they disregard and forget the nuances and recite them with the conviction of an apodictic and fatal proverb. Thus the idea they proclaim, which is a just psychological and moral observation, is transformed into a highly debatable historical assertion. Because, when all is said and done, is it possible that any past time was better than our own?

We could also say straight away that not everything

enters into Manrique's calculations. The supposition, the opinion, of the superiority of the ancient world, of any form of life surpassing another, is a cliché which is easy to track down throughout the centuries in the maxims and reflections of ascetics and moralists. People throughout all ages have had the weakness to believe that their own time, which it has been their fate to live through, was precisely a deplorable age. Phrases such as that of the gentle humanist Hutten, "It is good to be alive!", are not at all frequent in the memory of history; and I suspect that the majority of the contemporaries of the above-mentioned self-confessed optimist would not have subscribed to it. And the displeasure felt towards the present reality is unfailingly accompanied by a certain longing for the past, perhaps for any past. At the end of the day, it is perfectly understandable that it should be thus. We suffer the present time in all its severity: its inconveniences, even when they are only minimal, and they rarely are, become unavoidable for us. The past, on the other hand, is a simple memory, a pure illusion of the spirit, easily imaginable as more bearable or more benign than our grim present. The catastrophes and miseries of the past vanish, they remain neatly overlooked, and we limit ourselves to exclaiming, in yet another version of the cliché, "mais où sont les neiges d'antan?" There is yet more. From time to time, this type of romantic appreciation takes on the tone of a vast social judgment. There are many who consider that their time exceeds the depravity of that of their predecessors. The theory of a progressive dissipation of morals has throughout time and in all places had many followers. The past which nostalgia evokes is more comfortable and more decent.

And yet... There was once an erudite Catalan who collected together and published a rich series of medieval documents, all of them testimony to drunken occurrences, and gave them a title of deliciously folkloric resonance: "Geese have always had beaks". And in effect, geese have always had beaks and people have always had the same defects. We shall leave to one side for the moment the question as to whether the past, any past, was more comfortable than the present. There can be no doubt, however, that as far as decency is concerned more or less everything went according to style. Nor were the periods of intense religious saturation any exception, such as that which is called the Christian Middle Ages. With regard to a few important and basic aspects, men and women have behaved in almost the same way in the most diverse and separate places and moments of their societies. Human conduct is a tiring monotony. Clothes, institutions, economic and religious structures, anything you like, all change; but in essence, the inhabitants of the planet Earth repeat certain identical, unalterable clichés of crime and pleasure. Given that we are relying here on foreigners, I find in the *Guzmán de Alfarache* of Mateo Alemán this perfectly exact statement of fact: "Todo ha sido, es y será una misma cosa. El primero padre fue alevoso. La primera madre, mentirosa. El primer hijo, ladrón y fratricida. ¿Qué hay ahora que no hubo? ¿O qué se espera de lo por venir?"[8] Adam, Eve and Cain are perfectly good examples of what the Castilian novelist intended to insinuate.

I should like to suppose that Mateo Alemán would not have been scandalised to have read a book by Henry Miller — one of the *Tropics* — not to mention one of those insipid little narrations by Françoise Sagan. The appalling collection of obscenity and brutality which Curzio Malaparte so carefully prepared in *Kaputt* or *La pelle* would not surprise those who are a little up to date on the habits and inclinations of other times. In any case, the difference between what came before and that which we have today can be found to lie simply in the degree of publicity which we give nowadays to those episodes. There remains only a weak echo of tittle-tattle, a few documentary references of the violent, lustful or erotic debauchery of an ancient character; regarding a similar example from the present time; on the other hand, subject matter is found in lavish articles in wide-selling magazines, and the plots of films such as *La*

179

dolce vita. Finally, we should not think that we are more cynical than our predecessors. The ancients would have behaved the same way as us if they had possessed the means. They did not film *La dolce vita* but they wrote the *Satyricon*; it all amounts to the same thing, once distance has been overcome. On the other hand, if we are going to be concrete, it is necessary to examine whether our age is more cynical — in the denigrating sense which this word usually has — than others, or if it is simply more sincere.

Whatever the answer, the point is this. Reading the satirical authors of any time is very enlightening. In every mockery exists the rigorous desire to correct that which gave rise to it. It amounts to saying that every satirical author is a moralist. And, consequently, a realist. The most exact portraits of a society tend to be those provided by satirical writers. They exaggerate: caricature is their technique. But from this exaggeration, from this carica- ture, arises a true impression of a concrete society. Those familiar with the works of Aristotle, Martial, of our Jaume Roig and of the Valencian notaries and canons of the fif- teenth centuries, of Rabelais, of the Spanish picaresque, would arrive at the conclusion that, with regard to that which we call evil, humanity has a fairly limited capacity for invention. The vices censured by the shameless pen of Aristophanes (if the Greeks actually wrote with pens, something which I cannot claim to know), we find again inserted in the glorious psychological subtleties of Proust. No, we cannot deny that humanity has demonstrated sen- sational aptitudes; it has thought up philosophies like that of Hegel, machines like the *sputnik*, sciences as complex as those which are practised in foreign universities, atomic bombs, supermarkets, refrigerators, televisions, Kafka, and so many more. All grouped together, they form a very illustrious legacy. At any rate, no new mortal sin has been added to the short-list which is in the Catechism, nor will it be. Constancy can be stubborn in the extreme. My words are certainly not a reprimand. I am not in the least inter- ested in the invention of new sins. On the contrary, I am of the opinion that everyone would be better off were we to succeed in doing away with one or more of those which are presently in force. But is such a thing practical? The members of Mateo Alemán's family would say not. And I would not answer yes; I would be satisfied with giving a vote of confidence to the future. This I do.

WAR

I don't know what must have happened in times past. But contemporary history informs us that the masses have not been slow to go to war when their political masters have led them. Logically, the reverse should have occurred: as time wore on, the people, the great mass forming the population of various states, suffered more harshly from the consequences of any armed conflict as the capacity for destruction of the weapons at their disposal became progressively greater; and, at the same time, the possibilities for civilian action and collective awareness expanded among those self-same levels of society predestined to become victims. I mean that, weighing it all up, nations have been more and more in a position to realise that war is wicked and to act in order to prevent it. Yet the reaction of the masses at key moments has lain in the opposite direction: the people have shown themselves enthusiasts for war. Speaking of enthusiasm may seem an exaggeration. But I think we must call it that. It is obviously not unanimous but just as obviously felt by the majority. Propagandistic incitement, flag-waving opiate, deliberate deception (or self-deception?), it doesn't matter.

While readily admitting the influence of those factors, we must mention a further one: the fascination always aroused by the fact or possibility of a liberating break in the routine of the average person. The idea that the average person — this abstraction we refer to as the average person, an abstraction which is perfectly and statistically verifiable on empirical grounds — is a sensible, peaceable soul cannot be contested. But it's also true that the average person feels a kind of tedium or disgust, in the long term, with common sense and peace. Deep inside, people yearn for adventure, for a chance to unleash their darkest, most pathetic energies. In times of peace and civilian calm, this yearning is satisfied with violent books, gestures and spectacles which release them from repressions, albeit on a purely imaginative or imaginary plane — novels about gangsters, adventure films, boxing matches, driving too fast, seeking escape through alcohol or sensuality in measured doses. War opens up the gates to a more tangible expression of all this; struggle is scandalously well suited to providing the anarchic satisfaction sought by the individual. Since those who, in principle, have to wage war are the young, this tendency is accentuated in terms of romantic euphoria.

When war breaks out, it seems like a glorious holiday, during which everything will be permitted — and paid for. If subsequently this is proved wrong by the facts, and the macabre side of the conflict takes over, the enthusiasm and its wake of sentiment do not disappear. Soldiers sing when they leave for the front. Their song may at times be forced; often it's sincere. The words speak of the motherland, the enemy, victory. The music, in covert fashion, speaks of other ambitions: rape, pillage, slaughter and idleness. We would be incapable of understanding the history of the nineteenth and twentieth centuries, insofar as this history records the details of battles and the fervour of the combatants, were we to forget this tangible truth. War, in itself, is an intoxicating category.

WICKEDNESS
It's rather funny really: we are never as wicked as we think.

XENOPHOBIA

Hatred of foreigners, of strangers, has always and in all places been the cause of great acts of stupidity and sublime decisions, of savage crimes and wonderful poetry, of sacred sacrifice and worthwhile abuses. There are many forms of patriotism which are nothing more than xenophobia: in that it is often the case that the inhabitants of one country only begin to feel patriotic when they imagine or find themselves in conflict with a neighbouring country. Whatever the case, the foreigner is a polemical point of reference and probably indispensable for aggressive patriotism. Given that such strangers are also usually patriots of their own country and possess a similar attitude towards it, the collision ends up being fatal. Every xenophobia answers another xenophobia since we are all foreigners to somebody. And we make an enemy of the foreigner: every foreigner is a potential enemy. Only the modern expansion of tourism begins to abolish this principle of old, sentimental ancestry: now foreigners present themselves to us as customers. I do not know if tourism will end up taking the edge off xenophobia but I doubt it. The history of all nations gives long lists of heroic acts perpetrated by natives against foreigners and it is with these sorts of reminiscences that schoolteachers educate their pupils. The ignominious aspect which these acts can present is automatically explained away by the virtue of patriotism. Monsieur Chauvin is a dangerous animal but also a comforting reservoir of energy. I personally believe that the whole thing is basically deplorable. The appearances of the present world reveal, if not a dizzying decline in xenophobia, then an attenuation of its risks regarding the possibility of war. At least in large areas of the planet, the antagonism

184

which offers possibilities of a tragic outcome is now not between two peoples but rather between systems. Certainly on this new level, the same phenomenon, to put it in different terms, is repeated: a kind of class xenophobia, with a new dialectic but not entirely different in its consequences. The old xenophobia, the authentic xenophobia, the hatred towards strangers, still continues all the same and it will endure for a long time yet. Even if the state does institute an open system of education...

ZERO

Who, except for a person of immeasurable imagination, would be capable of imagining the idea of zero? I say *imagine* an *idea*. Obviously, great intellectual activity is required to attain it. This, only the mathematicians can do. Zero — nullity — nothingness? We make fun of philosophers, but what about the mathematicians?

Notes

[1] The Romantic re-awakening of interest in the cultural personality of Catalonia generally considered to date from Aribau's (1798-1862) poem La Pàtria published in 1833.

[2] The revolts of the *Germanies* in Valencia and Majorca of the early sixteenth century, the *Segadors* in Catalonia during the War of Thirty Years and the support for the Habsburg candidate over the Bourbon pretender in the War of Spanish Succession (1714) are prime examples of Catalan discontent at the erosion of their national liberties and centralist intrusion.

[3] Josep Pla (1897-1981) a popular journalist and essayist, much revered for his numerous writings on Catalonia and its people.

[4] Eugeni d'Ors (1881-1954) a celebrated cultural ideologue who wrote under the pseudonym of Xènius. Founder of the official aesthetic of *Noucentisme* (1906-1923) patronised by the ruling nationalist party he later abandoned Barcelona and reneged on his Catalanist affiliations.

[5] Disdain for the court and praise for the countryside.

[6] Gregorio Marañón (1887-1960) distinguished intellectual, pioneering endochrinologist and medical reformer.

[7] All time past was better.

[8] All was, and will ever be, the same. The first father was a traitor. The first mother, a liar. The first son, a thief and fratricide. Is there anything now that did not exist before? And what can be expected of the future?

Joan Fuster: a short biography

Joan Fuster was born in Sueca, a small rural town to the south of Valencia, on the 23rd of November 1922. His family was of peasant stock though his father became a trades- man and maker of religious statues. After a standard secondary education, Fuster started a course in Law at Valencia University in 1943 combining his studies with the odd foray into journalism which would incline him towards the profession of critic and columnist in later life. Despite the official proscription of Catalan, his first article in this language was published the following year and his literary vocation was cemented between 1946 and 1956 when he worked as co-editor of the review *Verbo*. After graduating in 1947 he practised as a lawyer in his native town — where he was to reside the rest of his life — though his legal career gave way in due course to a full- blooded commitment to scholarship.

Fuster's first major literary publications were in the field of poetry: *Sobre Narcís*/Upon Narcissus (1949), *Ales o mans*/Wings or Hands (1949), *Terra en la boca*/Earth in the Mouth (1953) i *Escrit per al silenci*/Written for Silence (1954), all of which would later appear in collected form in *Set llibres de versos*/Seven Books of Verse (1987). In 1954 his first collection of essays appeared, *El descrèdit de la realitat*/ Discrediting Reality, which heralded a brilliant career in the genre. There followed a series of major academic mono- graphs on the history, literature and language of Valencia which were to enhance the investigative stature of this indi- vidual passionately engaged with the Catalan nation, its nature and origins, social peculiarity and politics.

Throughout his career Fuster was forced to negotiate a whole sea of troubles: dictatorship, censorship, official dis- content and exclusion — not to mention the entire lack of cultural infrastructure and resources. In this ethos his work acquired a dimension of immense proportions and converted him in the 1960s into the great apologist for national aspirations in the face of the anti-democratic repression of the regime. In 1962 he published *Nosaltres, els valencians*/We Valencians, a *sine qua non* for the understanding of the problematic historical identity of Valencia within the Catalan configuration. The monograph established his credentials as an academic though, as was to be expected, the survey proved anathema to the Francoist establishment and the local Right. So extreme was their reaction that, during the city's annual festivities (*falles*) of the following year, an effigy of the writer was publicly burnt at the stake.

After the demise of the dictator the contribution of this intellectual was recognised institutionally. In 1975 Fuster was awarded the Premi d'Honor de les Lletres Catalanes and in 1983 he was appointed to a lectureship at Valencia University, receiving in the same year the Gold Medal of the Catalan Government. In 1984 he received an honorary doctorate from both Barcelona Universities and was elected to a chair in Catalan Literature in Valencia. The honours continued to accrue though, from this moment until his death in Sueca on June 21, 1992, Fuster preferred to avoid social protagonism and concentrate instead on research.

The resentment felt by the more hysterical elements of neo-Francoist inspiration were always to pursue the writer. In 1981 a bomb, the work of local right-wing militants, was planted in his house causing considerable damage though miraculously those inside escaped injury. Even today the figure of this intellectual is still anathema to local conservatism and in September 1997 his grave was desecrated although responsibility for the act was never attributed. In 1993 the Joan Fuster chair was created by the University of Valencia in order to honour the memory of this scholar and the immensity of his contribution to Catalan culture.

Translators' Note

The translation of this book was carried out by a team of academics from the Anglo-Catalan Society: Sally Anne Kitts, John-Pau Rubiés, Max Wheeler, Judith Willis, Alan Yates and Dominic Keown. The original text appeared in 1964 and our translation is based on the thirteenth edition of 2001 in the series *El Cangur* of Edicions 62, Barcelona, a reprographic version of the first edition. As a general rule we have tried to avoid burdening the reader with footnotes and have only used these when the reference is to a particular feature of Catalan culture which may be unknown. We have resisted the temptation to translate those passages quoted in other languages — mainly French — in order to equate the experience of the English reader with their Catalan counterpart. Evidently, given the alphabetic vagaries of these two languages, the order in which the definitions in each text appear will differ significantly.

The Editor

Dominic Keown is Reader in Catalan Studies at Fitzwilliam College, Cambridge. He has translated a number of Catalan writers — Salvat-Papasseit, March, J.V. Foix — and the Spanish playwright Valle Inclán and published monographs on contemporary Catalan culture, politics and film.

The Anglo-Catalan Society

The Anglo-Catalan Society was founded in 1954 in Oxford and exists to encourage cultural relations between the two linguistic communities and to promote awareness and appreciation of Catalan culture in the British Isles. While the Society serves as a professional forum for those involved in the teaching of Catalan studies, equal importance is attached to the role of bringing together Catalans and 'Catalanophiles'. In 1980 the society initiated a series of Anglo-Catalan Society Occasional Publications. The objective is to present the research and views of specialists, in the areas of Catalan society, history, language and culture, in a form of interest to scholars and general readers alike. The Society intends to publish material in electronic and paper formats and welcomes proposals. (www.anglo-catalan.org)

The Joan Fuster Chair was created by the University of Valencia in 1993 with the aim of promoting the work of this intellectual and fostering scholarship on his particular interests within Social Sciences and the Humanities. Such initiatives include the annual Fuster Symposium in Sueca, the bi-annual Fuster Award for research into his specialist areas, round tables, re-editions of his works and correspondence, exhibitions and lectures. A series of monographs is also published under the aegis of this chair by the University of Valencia.
More information: www.uv.es/catedra/val/index.htm

VNIVERSITAT ID VALENCIA

The **Institut Ramon Llull's** mission is to promote Catalan language and culture internationally, in all of its variations and methods of expression.
More information: www.llull.com

191

Other Catalan books by Five Leaves

CATALONIA

Catalonia is a comprehensive review of Catalan history and culture from its classical and medieval origins to the Universal Forum of Cultures 2004. John Payne's personal tone brings alive highlights of Catalan history and leading personalities of its cultural life. The book covers key periods in Catalan history from Greek and Roman times to the Spanish Civil War and modern times, including the mingling of Christian, Jewish and Muslim heritage and the popular street culture of processions, dancing and fireworks. Naturally, the author discusses Barcelona's extraordinary profusion of modern design and architecture, as well as aspects of Catalan life, language, environment and politics.

John Payne has lived and worked in Catalonia and visits regularly. He speaks both Catalan and Spanish, and is the author of *Journey Up the Thames: William Morris and Modern England*, published by Five Leaves, and *Catalonia: portrait of a nation*. He lives near Bath, and is a freelance researcher.

328pp   ISBN: 0 907123 29 5   £9.99

BARCELONA

Barcelona is one of Europe's most fashionable tourist destinations, blending the old and the new: model developments alongside mediaeval twisting alleys. This is the city evoked by its emblematic artists and writers — famous foreigners like Jean Genet and George Orwell and locals such as Manuel Vázquez Montalbán and Mercè Rodereda. This city — down at heel in the 60s — was dramatically re-invented as the glittering 1990s city of art and good living, and is claimed as a sustainable city of the twenty-first century. This book explains the transformation and questions its high claims. *Barcelona* is about the bustle of the *Rambles*, decadent Chinatown, *Art nouveau* buildings, festivals, food, a football club, Franco, Gaudí, the past and the future.

Michael Eaude has lived in Barcelona for sixteen years working as a freelance writer for the British and Spanish press and as a translator of Catalan and Spanish. He is the author of a book, in Spanish, on the novelist Arturo Barea and is active in Barcelona's huge anti-war and anti-globalisation movements.

322pp   ISBN: 1 905512 04 X   £9.99

FIVE LEAVES' TITLES ARE AVAILABLE FROM BOOKSHOPS OR, POST FREE, FROM:

FIVE LEAVES, PO BOX 8786, NOTTINGHAM NG1 9AW